Redeemed Like David

How to Overcome Sexual Temptation

By Mark Ballenger

Unless otherwise noted, all Scripture references are from the ESV.

For more books and resources by Mark Ballenger, please visit AGW Ministries at ApplyGodsWord.com.

ISBN-13:
978-1533681331

ISBN-10:
1533681333

This book is dedicated to my son, Logan David Ballenger.

Son, despite all of King David's failures, he always repented and sought the grace of God. This is what made him great. You can be great too.

Table of Contents

Preface

This journey is about you finally being free from the chronic, sexual temptations that have plagued you throughout your life. The road we will be following on this journey is Psalm 51. It was written by a man who knew the extreme freedom found in living for God but who also experienced the extreme shame that accompanies failure to sexual temptation.

King David, perhaps the most polarizing figure in all the Old Testament, lived a life full of the highest of highs and lowest of lows. Great military victories, shocking military defeats, thrilling times of Spirit led worship, overwhelming seasons of depression, fame, betrayal, political power, family love, family coups, awesome riches, beautiful women, amazing friendships, astonishing failures, sin, and heart wrenching personal losses – David lived through it all.

David's life is so varied, at some point it seems to resemble every person's life. Whether you are a rock star or you are the very definition of an average Joe, David could relate. And, like rock stars and average men alike, David had massive failures in the area of his sexuality too.

As unique as every person's life will be, every one of us has some form of failure with sexual temptation. What's different about David is that even though he got caught in the snares of sexual lust, David, unlike the majority, found his way out and overcame it. Despite all his massive failures, in the end, David was still remembered by the Lord as a man after God's own heart (Acts 13:22).

Clearly there is much to learn from King David. Like a young general seeking counsel from an older general who has seen far more battles and lived to speak about it, if we pay attention to what God showed David, we too can become warriors after God's own heart and overcome sexual temptation. The journey was not easy for David, and it certainly won't be easy for us, but if we pick up our swords, the word of God, and we head into battle, determined to fight for our freedom or die trying, the victory will be ours through Christ.

So if you are ready to overcome the sexual sin and the shackles of shame that are causing you to waste your life, if you are done pretending like you can just keep trying the same old things and get different results, if you are done being a slave to sexual temptation – if you are finally ready to become the man or woman God has called you to be, then pray this pray with me:

Our Father,
Have mercy on me, according to your unfailing love. I am stuck, and I know that I can never get unstuck without you. Please grant me the power, the wisdom, and the passion to fight for the freedom you desire for me to have in Christ. I don't know how it's going to happen, but I believe that your grace is great enough to set my heart free from every sin, including sexual sin. I give you permission to break me so that you have the opportunity to remake me in your image. Whatever it takes to make me completely yours, please do it in me. Your will be done, O Father, for the sake of your great name. In the name and power of Jesus, alone, I do pray, Amen.

Introduction: Scandalous Sin Needs Scandalous Grace

Psalm 51: Intro
To the choirmaster. A Psalm of David, when Nathan the
prophet went to him, after he had gone in to Bathsheba.

God's grace given to us in the gospel of Jesus Christ is utterly scandalous. It really is an absurd gift.

Jesus, our perfect God, came down in human form, lived a perfect life, gave humans no reason to kill him, but we did, and then he says, "Grace . . . I give you grace. You sinned against me, but I'm going to love you. You were unfaithful to me, but I'm going to be faithful to you. You were my enemy, but I am going to die for you so you will be my Father's pure sons and daughters once again."

This is scandalous. Perhaps nowhere else is a picture of God's grace seen more clearly than in the life of David. If you're unfamiliar with David's story, it starts with God choosing and anointing him. He was the youngest in his family, the least deserving to be the king of Israel, but God chose him anyway. David then killed Goliath, fought and won many battles, and eventually became the most celebrated king of God's chosen people. Jesus' lineage can be traced back to David.

Despite all of this, right at the peak of his life, David totally and utterly blows it through sexual sin. He commits adultery with another man's wife, he has the husband murdered because the woman gets pregnant, and in the end, because of David's sin, the baby dies (2 Samuel 11-12). And then when David is long dead, he is remembered in Acts 13:22 to be "a man after God's own heart."

Wait . . . what? What! How can this be? How can this sinner, this adulterer, this murder, this fool who caused the death of an innocent baby – how can this man be so highly favored by such a holy God? This truly is scandalous grace.

To understand how all these pieces fit together, we have to take a long drive down Psalm 51. Psalm 51 is the missing key to understanding how David could go from being a rebel to a man redeemed, a man after God's own heart.

The Magnitude of David's Sin Reveals the Greatness of God's Mercy

David knew God in a special way, and yet David sinned horribly, probably far worse than anyone reading this book. So we can fully appreciate Psalm 51, let's review 2 Samuel 11:2-5 to give us a greater understanding of the sin David committed:

> "One evening David got up from his bed and walked around on the roof of the palace. From the roof he saw a woman bathing. The woman was very beautiful, and David sent someone to find out about her. The man said, "She is Bathsheba, the daughter of Eliam and the wife of Uriah the Hittite." Then David sent messengers to get her. She came to him, and he slept with her. (Now she was purifying herself from her monthly uncleanness.) Then she went back home. The woman

conceived and sent word to David, saying, "I am pregnant."

And there it is. Just the plain, raw, sinful facts. No punches pulled. No sugarcoating it. You don't have to guess at what happened. And as you read further it just keeps getting worse.

David doesn't instantly repent. He tries to make it right his own way. He tries to get Bathsheba's husband to sleep with her so it will seem like it's Uriah's baby. But Uriah won't cooperate. David then sends Uriah back to the front lines, and in a sickening twist to the plot, he actually sends a letter with Uriah to give to the commander of David's army with the instruction to put Uriah in the thick of the battle so he will die (2 Samuel 11:14-15).

To make matters worse, if that's possible, it's also worth noting that Uriah was actually a valiant warrior committed to David. They were probably close friends, which can be assumed since only friends of the king would have a house so close to the palace like Uriah and Bathsheba did. And Uriah was not just an average soldier. He was actually a member of David's "Might Men," one of "The Thirty" listed by name in 1 Chronicles 11:41.

These men were amongst David's most loyal warriors. In 1 Chronicles 12, David was pinned down by his enemy, and these mighty men, which included Uriah, came to David's rescue. When David saw the men, 1 Chronicles 12:17-18 explains:

> "David went out to meet them and said to them, 'If you have come to me in friendship to help me, my heart will be joined to you; but if to betray me to my adversaries, although there is no wrong in my hands, then may the God of our fathers see and rebuke you.' Then the Spirit clothed Amasai, chief of the thirty, and he said,
>
> 'We are yours, O David, and with you, O son of Jesse! Peace, peace to you, and peace to your helpers! For your God helps you.' Then David received them and made them officers of his troops."

David made these mighty men swear their allegiance to him. This was probably one of the reasons Uriah would not sleep with Bathsheba when David summoned him home as a cover for Bathsheba's pregnancy. 2 Samuel 11:10-11 reveals Uriah's loyalty to God, king, and country, which is a true mark of any good warrior:

> "When they told David, 'Uriah did not go down to his house,' David said to Uriah, 'Have you not come from a journey? Why did you not go down to your house?' Uriah said to David, "The ark and Israel and Judah dwell in booths, and my lord Joab and the servants of my lord are camping in the open field. Shall I then go to my house, to eat and to drink and to lie with my wife? As you live, and as your soul lives, I will not do this thing."

Additionally, Uriah knew that active soldiers were not to have sexual relations during a military campaign. Even with the blessing of David to do so, Uriah would not forsake his duty as a warrior. Uriah was clearly a good man, a good warrior, and a good friend.

How does David treat one of his "Mighty Men" and one of his most loyal soldiers? David simply pats Uriah on the back, hands him the letter with his death warrant in it, and sends this faithful man to walk back to his bloody end, "See ya, buddy-old-pal, my good and loyal friend . . . ."And then David marries Uriah's wife.

David's sexual sin just kept leading to more and more sin. The same is true for us. When we don't repent, our sins just get progressively worse and worse.

David Knew Better, Just Like We Know Better

These sins are horrible if anyone committed them, but the fact that King David committed these sins makes the offense all the more shocking.

If a professor of trigonometry blows 2+2, it is far worse than if a child who just learned to add gets it wrong. David was like a professor when it came to God's ways. He was like the dean of the seminary.

He knew God as much as anyone in the entire Bible ever did. He spent his nights alone as a boy being strengthened in the wilderness by God. He felt the anointing of God's Spirit. He felt the favor of God come on him during the battles. As king of Israel, David was actually required to write by hand God's entire law (Deuteronomy 17:18). This man truly knew God.

Check out the book of Psalms and you will find the majority of it was written by David; it is a book filled with verses referring to the intimacy David had with the LORD.

You see? What makes David's sexual sin with Bathsheba so bad is that he did it with eyes wide open. It's not like he broke some Levitical law buried deep in the Old Testament everyone forgot about. David knew 2+2 equals 4. He knew his spiritual ABC's: don't murder, don't commit adultery, don't lie, don't covet. Like all of us who struggle with sexual sin, David wasn't stupid, he was just sinful.

The Hebrew word for "transgressions" in Psalm51:1 denotes a willful deviation from the path of righteousness, a premeditated crossing over the line of God's law. The clearest proof of human depravity and sinfulness at the heart level is when we sin but know better. When we sin with full consciousness, with eyes wide open, this is what points to the depth of our fallenness like nothing else. It's one thing when you sin because you didn't know. The sin is on a much worse level of evil when we knew and we did it anyway.

Luke 12:48 states, "But the one who does not know and does things deserving punishment will be beaten with few blows. From everyone who has been given much, much will be demanded; and from the one who has been entrusted with much, much more will be asked." This truth applies to us all. We have all been given much. We can all relate to David who indulged in sexual sin with eyes wide open. And, like David, we all know from experience that the worst type of shame comes from the sexual sin that you committed even though you knew better.

If we hope that this journey leads to freedom, we have to start with being brutally honest with ourselves. We didn't just sin sexually. We spat in the face of God and turned our back on him with eyes wide open. You had sex before marriage like you knew you shouldn't have. You committed adultery even though you really do know how much your spouse loves you. You made the promise you would never lust after porn again, and then it happens again, the very next day. You got the abortion when you knew it was murder, and then you got another one. You made all the promises to God that you would never date another person like that and then somehow, a few months later, you end up dating the same type of person you know doesn't desire to please God. You went to the sex-addict meetings, you told yourself you'd never masturbate again, you got the counseling, you put the porn blockers up . . . but then failed again.

We didn't want any of this to happen, but it happened, so now what?

If God Redeemed David from Sexual Sin, He Can Redeem Us Too

What can we possibly do now? We must do what David did in Psalm 51. He doesn't make God a promise. Instead he bends his knees in prayer and relies completely on God's scandalous grace.

As we study these nineteen verses, the first thing we must do is capture the spirit in which they were written. David did not write a technical, psychology-saturated, step-by-step plan on how to overcome sexual temptation. David wrote Psalm 51 as a heart-felt prayer to God. He prayed as a man who knew he was in absolute desperate need.

We must study Psalm 51 prayerfully, knowing that it will not be through tips and techniques that we are set free from the snares of sexual bondage, but through God's amazing grace. God alone has the power to set us free. Therefore, like David, let's rely on God alone for the freedom we so desperately desire.

I highly doubt you have sinned in such dramatic ways as David. If God could redeem a man who failed in such massive ways, surely God can redeem us. Once David and Bathsheba were properly married, they had another son, Solomon. Out of all of David's others sons, even though Solomon was not the eldest, God chose him to be the king after David. Perhaps the reason God used Solomon was to show us all how God's grace truly is great enough to redeem any situation. Remember, God used David, a man with a truly messy sexual past, to start a lineage through which Jesus would eventually come.

God's scandalous grace was enough for David's sexual sin, and it is more than enough for ours as well.

Chapter 1: Freedom Always Starts With God

Psalm 51:1-2
Have mercy on me, O God, according to your steadfast love;
according to your abundant mercy blot out my transgressions.
² Wash me thoroughly from my iniquity, and cleanse me from
my sin!

If you're anything like me, when you make a mistake, the first thing you do is try to make it right. Maybe you do what we all did as little kids. When you hurt one of your friends or younger siblings, rather than let them get you in trouble, you offered them a deal, "Don't tell mom. Here, punch me back, pay me back." And then once they took their retribution, you made sure to over embellish how bad it actually hurt to ensure you would be dept free.

Psalm 51 does not start that way. If you do anything other than depend on Jesus Christ after you sin sexually, you are relying on something other than the power of God for your freedom. If you try doing something good to make up for what you did that was bad, you are relying on your works rather than God's grace.

David doesn't make promises to God. He doesn't try to cut a deal to pay for his sins. Instead he turns to God in prayer.

Freedom Road Starts With Forgiveness

Psalm 51:1, "Have mercy on me, O God . . . ."

David starts where we must all start if we hope to overcome sexual temptation. David is repenting, which means he is seeking to drive the other direction from his sin. He wants his life to change. He never wants to sin like this again. To accomplish this, David starts his journey by dealing with his past mistakes.

You will never be able to live free from future sexual temptation until you have first been forgiven of your past sexual sins. Sexual sin is bondage. It causes us to owe a debt we cannot pay. Sexual sin brings immense shame, and it ruins our future if the sins of the past are not dealt with first. A lack of feeling forgiven only perpetuates the deadly, endless cycle of sexual sin patterns: You feel horrible because of your sexual sin, but you are drawn to sexual sin because you feel horrible. To break the cycle, like David, we need to start with forgiveness.

You won't ever be forgiven of you sexual sin because you've fought to overcome it. Rather, you will only overcome sexual temptation once you are forgiven and thus freed. Freedom doesn't lead to forgiveness. Forgiveness leads to freedom. To overcome sexual sin in the future, Psalm 51:1-2 shows us that we must first be forgiven and set free from the sexual sins of our past.

The problem with this is that many of us won't trust God's forgiveness. After all, you've tried this before. This probably isn't the first time you've asked God to forgive you. It's hard to receive forgiveness when you have to ask again and again for the same problem over and over. We feel we've asked too many times, we've made too many broken promises, and therefore we've concluded our sexual sin is just too much.

It would be too much if God's love and forgiveness was based in us. Thankfully, it most definitely is not.

God's Scandalous Grace Is Rooted in God

Psalm 51:1, ". . . according to your steadfast love; according to your abundant mercy . . . ."

The Hebrew word for mercy used in Psalm 51:1 is "hanan" and in the Old Testament this word frequently appears in the context of the weak appealing to the strong. This same word is used in Ester 4:8 to describe how Ester was going to appeal to the king. Ester was going to "beg for mercy" on behalf of her people. The king had all the power to kill all the Jews and Ester had none, but Ester "begs for mercy."

David is appealing to God's mercy because David knew God had all the power to destroy him. David repents not by making promises. He repents by appealing to one more powerful than himself. David starts down the road of repentance the way everyone should. "Have mercy on me, O God, according to your steadfast love; according to your abundant mercy" basically summarizes all of Christianity. David is basically saying, "Give to me what only you have and what I don't deserve." Freedom's road always starts with asking for that which you don't deserve from the only One able to give it.

"Have mercy on me." Why? "Because of your unfailing love."
"Blot out my transgressions." Why? "Because of your great
compassion." What's David doing here? David is appealing to
the loving nature of God. David knows that when it comes to
rights, things deserved, things earned, and things owed by
God, he doesn't have a leg to stand on.

David knows that his only chance before God is God. He
knows that if ever the Lord is going to forgive him, it is going
to be because of the loving nature of God, not because of
something David might do or say.

David's not appealing to this past exploits. "Have mercy on
me, O God, according to the time I struck down Goliath. Blot
out my transgressions with Bathsheba according to all the
times I didn't commit adultery and murder someone's
husband. According to the temple I'm going to help my son
Solomon build for you, cleanse me from my sin."

No, David knows that if he is going to have any chance with
God, it is going to be on God's terms, because of God's grace,
because God has it within himself to forgive. No deals, no
bargains, no convincing . . . just straight, hardcore grace.

**God Doesn't Love Us Because We're Clean. He Cleans Us
Because He Loves Us**

Good parents don't love their baby because the baby is clean.
Parents clean their babies because of the parents' love.

Take it from me, if parents only loved clean kids, children
would be unlovable. My son is a gifted child. The messes he

makes are like a work of art. Sometimes he makes them so fast, and yet the attention to detail he takes in his destruction is still so obviously apparent, rather than scold him I just have to take a minute to admire his skill.

I remember even when he was just 5 months old I was astonished at how much of a mess this 17 pound baby could produce. He was constantly spitting up, filling his pants, peeing all over the place. I remember changing his diaper and while I was in between taking the old one off and putting the new one on, I wasn't quite fast enough. He decided he needed to cut loose, so that's what he did. The boy had such good aim and power behind it he peed all over the drapes on our windows next to the changing table. To this day I am certain it was intentional.

I remember years ago when I was first using this analogy for a sermon. Even as I was writing about him making a mess, Bethany (my wife) came running up to my office to show me another masterpiece. In those days he had a knack for pooping in such a way that his diaper was truly defenseless. A few times a day he would shoot it all the way up to his shoulder blades, just straight up his back . . . a total baby blow out. One time I came into the room and Bethany had pee on her shirt, puke in her hair, and she was holding another defeated diaper. So of course I went and got the camera . . . it was just too classic to miss.

So what's the point of my parenting tales: You don't love your children because they are clean. You clean them because you love them. And that's how God treats us. He doesn't love us because we are clean of sin. He cleanses of our sin because he loves us.

David prayed in Psalm 25:7, "Do not remember the sins of my youth and my rebellious ways; according to your love remember me, for you, LORD, are good." David appeals to the goodness of the Lord, not to his own sinful past. He's saying, "When you look at me, don't see me as I deserve to be seen. See me in accordance to your loving kindness. Wash me because of who you are."

God Doesn't Love Us Because of What We Do. He Loves Us Because of Who He Is

One of the most important principles you could ever know about the love God is this: God doesn't love you because of what you do. God loves you because of who he is. 1 John 4:16 states, "God is love." Romans 5:8 explains, "But God demonstrates his own love for us in this: While we were still sinners, Christ died for us."

God can love us even when we are his enemies because his love isn't based in us at all. It's based in him. God is the reason for God's unfailing love, not you or me or anything we did or didn't do. You can't lose the love of God because you never did anything to receive it in the first place. You can't let the love of God down because you were never holding it up.

Of course God hates our sin, but he doesn't hate us because we sin, just like he doesn't love us because we don't sin. You could never earn the love of God or lose the love of God because God's love is totally, unequivocally, absolutely, 100 percent based within himself because of who he is. It saves you, benefits you, but it does not nor will it ever originate with you. His love is a consuming fire that devours all that comes in its path, but it is fueled by God and God alone.

Our salvation was never based upon our lack of sin. Rather, our salvation is based upon the price paid by our Savior and the awesome power of our God. So no matter how miserably we fail, we can come back to God through Christ.

Jesus is our Savior because he has the power to save. Our worth, our forgiveness, our cleansing, our sanctification, our justification, and our eternal glorification in the age to come are because of Christ, through Christ, and for Christ. God is God with or without us; therefore he alone can handle our deepest failures and faults.

God Shows His Love Through Christ's Cleansing Blood

Psalm 51:1-2, ". . . blot out my transgressions. ²Wash me thoroughly from my iniquity, and cleanse me from my sin!"

David appeals to the great love and mercy of God, but David knows that God expresses his love not by overlooking our failures but by redeeming us. God expresses his love not by pardoning sin but by paying the debt of our sin.

David doesn't pray, "According your great compassion, overlook my sin this one time." He knew that just because God's love was unfailing, God's love does not cancel out the reality of God's holiness and justice. David repents not by simply asking to be pardoned but to have his sin blotted out so his relationship with God might be restored. He turns to the right person to have his sins blotted out, for God uses the same language to describe himself in Isaiah 43:25, "I, even I, am he who blots out your transgressions, for my own sake, and remembers your sins no more."

How does God blot out our sins? David probably didn't understand how God could blot out his sins, he just knew he could. He probably knew that animal sacrifices weren't enough, for in Psalm 51:16 David admits, "For you will not delight in sacrifice, or I would give it; you will not be pleased with a burnt offering."

David couldn't have fully understood how this great unfailing love and great abundant mercy of God would manifest. But on this side of the cross, we have the responsibility to view everything through the lens of Christ crucified and raised from the dead. In Romans 3:25 (NLT) Paul explains the sins of the Old Testament in light of what Christ did in the New Testament, "For God presented Jesus as the sacrifice for sin. People are made right with God when they believe that Jesus sacrificed his life, shedding his blood. This sacrifice shows that God was being fair when he held back and did not punish those who sinned in times past."

We have to get our theology right. God doesn't just sweep David's sins under the rug. He redeems David through the death and resurrection of Jesus Christ. He placed David's sins and all of our sins on Christ when our Savior hung on the cross for all wrong doings – past, present, and future.

Christ Is the Manifestation of God's Love and Mercy

To really understand David's words in Psalm 51:1-2, we need to have Jesus in our minds. Studying God's character is just an academic exercise until you put flesh on it. When you see the compassion of God in the Old Testament, you should picture Christ dying on the cross in the New Testament.

If I were to simply teach this Old Testament psalm without ever mentioning what happened to Jesus in the New Testament, this would not be a Christian message. For something to be Christian, Christ has to be at the center of it. If I don't point to the cross a Muslim, Mormon, or Jew might read this book and say, "Fine job, Mark. I and my religion agree." Unlike other religions, the whole Bible teaches us that in Christianity, all reconciliation, all forgiveness, and all grace is totally dependent upon Christ and his gospel.

Colossians 1:15 says, "He [Jesus] is the image of the invisible God." The implications of this verse are staggering. This means that the invisible God David is pleading with, who is full of compassion and full of unfailing love, is manifested to the human eye through Jesus.

The manifestation of God's "steadfast love" and "abundant mercy" is pictured for the world to see no longer in animal sacrifice or simply in words on a page. God's quality of unfailing love and great compassion mentioned in Psalm 51:1-2 are now to be seen through and in Christ.

If you wonder how great the love of God really is, wonder no more. Just read Matthew, Mark, Luke and John and find out for yourself what "God is love" really means by witnessing the life of Christ. The love of God finds its meaning and is pictured most clearly in the life, death, and resurrection of Jesus – in the gospel of Jesus Christ, our only Savior. Jesus said to his disciple, "Don't you know me, Philip, even after I have been among you such a long time? Anyone who has seen me has seen the Father" (John 14:8-9).

 Without the image of Jesus to help us understand the invisible qualities of God, it would be like a person who never saw the night sky full of stars because they lived in a cave and only got to read about the stars in books. The descriptions would be wonderful to someone who had never seen the night sky full of stars. Explaining how all the gases and chemical reactions create light all over the night sky would be marvelous. But to one day step out of that dark cave and see all the galaxies and stars shining in all their glory would bring them to their knees.

Likewise, reading about God's love is wonderful. And yet, when we come to know Jesus, the full image of God is seen and this impacts our life in an everlasting way. Hebrews 1:1-3 (NIV) explains:

> "In the past God spoke to our ancestors through the prophets at many times and in various ways, but in these last days he has spoken to us by his Son, whom he appointed heir of all things, and through whom also he made the universe. The Son is the radiance of God's glory and the exact representation of his being, sustaining all things by his powerful word. After he had

provided purification for sins, he sat down at the right hand of the Majesty in heaven."

David wasn't forgiven because of the skill of his repentance. He wasn't forgiven because he killed a few animals and went to the temple to worship. He was forgiven because of Christ crucified. And this is the only reason we can be forgiven as well.

God only blots out our sin through the blood of Christ (John 14:6). If you have a great dept you cannot pay, you better have some rich friends. God is the only one with enough grace to handle our massive guilt. Mercy is always paid for in blood. What we've done is not greater than who Christ is. David is not the hero of the story. Jesus is always the hero. What made David great was his reliance on God's character. We can be great too, despite all our failures, if we rely not on ourselves but on who God is.

Our relationship starts with God, is sustained by God, and will continue on because of God. Therefore, this day, this week, this month, this year, and throughout your whole life, when you sin and turn from God, because you will, we all will, remember this: God can handle it. Freedom starts with forgiveness, so always return to God and seek his forgiveness.

If you don't think God can handle you and your sinful past, present, and future, your view of God is too small. Our God is larger and has more "steadfast love" and "abundant mercy" than you or I will ever know. But what we do know can be seen most clearly in Christ.

To live free and overcome sexual sin, we must look to Christ in all things.

Going Deeper

1. What's typically your first reaction after you commit a sexual sin?

2. What should be your first reaction after you commit a sexual sin?

3. What sin cycles have you been trapped in? Do you sin, feel shame, stay away from God, and then sin more because you are staying away from God? Or do you have a different sin pattern? How can you break your specific sin cycle?

4. How do our past sexual failures affect our ability to fight sexual temptation in the future? Do you believe forgiveness of our past will lead to freedom in the future?

5. Do you feel it is important to immediately repent after you sin rather than letting time go by? Why or why not?

6. Why is it essential to know that God's love and mercy are based in God's character and not our character?

7. If someone asked you, "What does the love of God look like?" how would you answer?

8. What person in your life have you felt the most loved by? Why has his or her love impacted you more than others?

9. When you struggle to receive God's forgiveness, is it because you think your sin is too big or because you think God is too small or a combination of both? How can you combat these false beliefs? (See Romans 8:31-39)

10. Psalm 51:2 (ESV) states, "Wash me thoroughly from my iniquity." Psalm 51:2 (NIV) states, "Wash away all my iniquity." It says God can wash us "thoroughly" and he can wash away "all" our sins. Is there any specific sexual sin or reoccurring sin in your past or present that you feel God cannot forgive? If so, apply the truths we've been studying in this passage. Confess it to God and believe his love, mercy, and grace are greater than all your failures.

Chapter 2: Convicted But Not Condemned

Psalm 51:3
For I know my transgressions, and my sin is ever before me.

When I hear a rattling under my car, as much as I like to hope, that rattle never seems to go away on its own. No matter how much I turn up my music, the problem just keeps getting louder.

My wife is much better at this. When she gets in the car and hears the breaks rubbing, she calls the mechanic right away. I'm usually waiting a few more weeks to make that call because you never know, the breaks may have just gotten wet, so . . . maybe they are screeching because they're a little moist. Hey, don't judge. It's possible. Right?

I remember the days when I was single, before my wife brought some wisdom into my life. My dashboard always reminded me of a Christmas tree. I would have the red "Check Brakes" light on, the green "Door Adjure" light, the yellow blinking "Need Gas" light, and of course the classic orangish-yellow "Check Engine" light.

Back then I knew even less about cars than I do now, but I did know that sometimes warning lights were just because of a faulty censor. This was a fact I liked to remind myself of often, "Oh, it's all probably just a bad censor. Once I start going up a hill the gas idle will rise again." Thankfully I had a very kind dad who was gracious enough to pick me up on the side of the road once every few months.

As much as Bethany has helped me act more like a responsible adult, I'm still a work in progress. The worst example of my self-inflicted optimism was when the birds got into our attic. It's a finished attic with a drywall ceiling. Awhile back I thought I heard some scratching noises and perhaps some small chirps. In classic fashion, I wanted to ignore the problem rather than deal with it.

I told myself the birds were probably just on the roof. Eventually the chirps got louder and there were more of them. Bethany finally heard them and encouraged me to do something about it. Of course I began to make excuses in my mind, "Okay, well they may be in the attic ceiling. But, hey, they got in themselves, so I'm sure they'll get out themselves too."

Well they didn't. Instead it seemed more were finding their way in. Or perhaps a family of distant relatives all decided to hatch their eggs together in my attic ceiling. It seems the word got around town in the bird community, "Hey, we found this warm place where no responsible humans are bothering us. Follow me." It eventually got so bad that my family and I could be two floors away in our living room and still hear the birds singing a group melody. It was like we had a bird exhibit upstairs. I considered charging admission to all the local bird watchers, "For just $5, come and hear the chirps of every bird species in Ohio." I often try to use humor as a cover for my negligence. Bethany wasn't laughing.

That's what happens when we deny our sexual sin issues. They start small. A little chirp here, a little chirp there. They stay in the corner of your house, in the attic, in the closet, away from the rest of the family . . . for awhile. As time goes on, however, sexual sin always get worse and it starts seeping out into the rest of your life and those closest to you begin to take notice.

Eventually sexual sin gets so bad that no matter what room you try to hide in to overlook your problem, you, your family, and your friends will no longer be able to ignore the sounds coming from the rooms you've neglected. When ignored, sexual sin multiplies like the birds in my attic and eventually it will overtake your whole house, affecting your quality of living no matter where you go.

When we are not honest about our problems, sin just get worse. It's a popular saying, "Time is the great healer." Not when it comes to sin it isn't. Sexual sin is a predator, looking to devour all that it can. If you don't admit that it's hunting you, you're just going to get eaten.

God Does Not Condemn or Condone a Christian's Sin, But He Does Convict

Psalm 51:3, "For I know my transgressions, and my sin is ever before me."

If you choose to deny your disease, you will also ignore the Cure, Christ Jesus.

It's crucial to notice that the first word in Psalm 51:3 is "For." This word is like "because." This means that what was said in

Psalm 51:1-2 is being said "because" of the truth found in Psalm 51:3.

David pleaded for mercy and love because of God's loving and merciful nature, but he would never have done this action if he was not first convicted of his sin. Psalm 51:2 says, "Wash me thoroughly from my iniquity, and cleanse me from my sin!" Why? Psalm 51:3 explains, "For I know my transgressions, and my sin is ever before me." If you don't come to grips with how evil your sexual sin really is, you will never truly cry out to God for deliverance.

There is a very big biblical difference between conviction and condemnation for Christians. To be condemned is to be found guilty and sentenced to punishment. The condemned must pay the dept. Thankfully, through the gospel of Jesus Christ, for those of us who receive God's grace purchased for us on the cross, we don't ever have to be condemned again. Romans 8:1 assures us, "There is therefore now no condemnation for those who are in Christ Jesus."

God may not condemn Christians, but he certainly does not condone our sexual sin either. Rather than condemning or condoning our sexually rebellious ways, God desires to bring a holy conviction. God knows no one will pray like David did in Psalm 51:1-2 if they are not first convicted of their sin like David was in Psalm 51:3.

If a deep conviction over sexual sin is needed to repent passionately like David finally did, how do we find this conviction?

The Holy Spirit Convicts Us Through God's Word

Father, Son, and Holy Spirit are all one, they are all God, and yet all three are distinct persons with different roles. One of the roles of the Holy Spirit is to bring conviction over sin. The Holy Spirit's conviction saves us from God's eternal condemnation. Jesus explained:

> "And when he [the Holy Spirit] comes, he will convict the world concerning sin and righteousness and judgment . . . When the Spirit of truth comes, he will guide you into all the truth, for he will not speak on his own authority, but whatever he hears he will speak, and he will declare to you the things that are to come. (John 16:8, 13)

The Holy Spirit certainly speaks to us personally, but whenever he speaks it always corresponds and never contradicts God's written word. The Holy Spirit does not speak "new" revelations to Christians, but he does apply the Bible to our lives in new and personal ways. The Bible is inspired by the Holy Spirit, which means that the Holy Spirit used the hands of men to write his own words (Mark 12:36, 2 Peter 1:21).

So what does this mean for overcoming sexual sin? This means that the Holy Spirit will always convict us of sin and move us towards repentance through what he has spoken in the Bible.

Notice that David was not convicted of his sin until Nathan the prophet came and spoke with him. Before Psalm 51:1, the Scriptures have given us the background information and setting of Psalm 51 in a brief introduction, "To the choirmaster. A Psalm of David, when Nathan the prophet went to him, after he had gone in to Bathsheba."

In the times of David, much of the Old Testament was still being written and formed. Today God reveals his final word through the Bible, applying it through the Holy Spirit in a personal way. In David's day, God's authoritative and final words were spoken through the prophets, of whom Nathan was one. Therefore, when David was confronted by Nathan, it was like when we are confronted by the pages of Scripture.

2 Samuel 12 is where David finally comes to his senses and begins to repent, turning back to God. The chapter begins with, "And the LORD sent Nathan to David" (1 Samuel 12:1). Only God can send a deep and true repentance. Only he can give us this gift. He alone can awaken the dead, bring feeling to the numb, and make us hate what we formerly idolized. We must pray to God that he brings a holy conviction to our life that moves us to a passionate hatred of sexual sin and towards a relentless pursuit of purity in Christ.

Again, only God can bring us the conviction we need, but when God does bring conviction, he always uses the Bible. If we want the conviction and a sincere disdain for disobeying God, we must spend massive amounts of time in God's word.

Perhaps the reason you are stuck in your sexual sin is because the word of God is not in you. You may be saved, the Holy Spirit may be dwelling in you, but you also need to actively hide the word of God in your heart. When you spend time in God's word, the holiness of it rebels when unholy temptations draw near. Conviction of sin is a reaction of the holiness and truth within you towards evil when it draws near. Truth and lies cannot coexist. The more light you put into your life, the easier it will be to spot darkness and keep it away.

If you have God's word hidden in your heart, you will have pings of inner pain when your heart begins to stray towards sexual sin. Without regularly feeding your heart truth, you will have less and less conviction over sexual sin. Without conviction, godly guilt, and holy remorse over sexual sin, we will never repent like David.

Psalm 119:9 affirms this truth, "How can a young man keep his way pure? By guarding it according to your word." If we want to be redeemed and set free from sexual sin like David, then we must be convicted by God's word like David.

The Holy Spirit Convicts Us Through the Church (and Accountability Partners)

If we are not willing to be honest, God won't make us holy. Honesty goes hand in hand with holiness. Denial of sin always translates into death.

In addition to bringing conviction through God's word, the Holy Spirit also brings conviction through the Church. By the Church I mean other Christians with which you have a committed relationship. David had a relationship with Nathan and Nathan was clearly a man who desired to please God. If you want to be sexually pure, then you must surround yourself with other people who have the same goals.

There has been a lot said over the years about "accountability partners," and I could say a lot more. Rather than explain the minute details of this relationship, perhaps it would be more helpful to simply give a few words of counsel and warning. The person every Christian is ultimately accountable to is God. God, however, often uses his Church to discipline Christians (1 Corinthians 5). So there is a place to be disciplined by others.

However, church discipline is for those Christians who are living in unrepentant sins. Accountability partners do more harm than good when Christians build a relationship revolving around sin checking. The relationships that help us the most are the relationships that help us focus more and more on Christ, not our sin. Most accountability partners don't last long because God did not design us to be each other's prison wardens.

Accountability partners, therefore, should keep each other accountable not so much about what they are avoiding but on what they are pursuing. It's far more helpful to encourage each other in your love for Christ, passion for growing closer to God through his word, desire to pray, and your desire to seek purity.

Additionally, the fear of embarrassing yourself to another person is not great enough to keep you from sinning. The only thing a relationship centered on sin checking will do is ruin the friendship or cause the two of you to lie. There certainly comes a time when a good friend should confront another friend about sin. Confronting a brother or sister in Christ about their sin, however, is the overflow of a good friendship, not the foundation of a good friendship. Proverbs 27:6, "Faithful are the wounds of a friend . . . ." If you want an accountability partner, you first need a good friend. Good, godly friends are produced through seeking and serving Jesus Christ together, not through calling someone once week you barely know to ask about their sexual sin.

Knowing you are going to have to tell someone you committed sexual sin sounds like a healthy safeguard, but sexual sin is way more powerful than your fear of other people. Only a love and healthy fear of God is powerful enough to be a successful weapon against sexual sin. David emphasizes this point in Psalm 51:4.

Going Deeper

1. Are you convicted about your sexual sin? Why or why not?

2. How does the word of God help bring a healthy conviction?

3. How does the Church and other Christians help bring conviction?

4. Do you see the benefits of having what has commonly been called an "accountability partner"? Do you see any potential problems that can happen within this relationship? Lastly, if you've had an accountability partner before, what were some good and bad lessons you learned about this type of relationship through your past experiences?

5. How can you find other people in your life who can help you pursue Christ and fight sexual temptation?

6. Have you ever ignored the Holy Spirit's conviction? What happened?

7. If you don't believe something is wrong, you won't have conviction over it. Is there a sin in your life you don't think is really that bad or actually wrong? What does the Bible say about this?

8. How can you tell the difference if you are feeling condemned or feeling convicted? What can you do to reject false feelings of condemnation while being careful not to ignore the feelings of conviction?

9. We all struggle to read God's word at certain times in life. To help bring motivation, list 10 benefits of regularly reading the Bible.

10. No matter where you are at with receiving the Holy Spirit's conviction, we can always be more sensitive to his leading. Write out a prayer asking the Holy Spirit to bring a holy conviction over your sexual sin.

Chapter 3: Those Who Are Forgiven Much, Love Much

Psalm 51:4
Against you, you only, have I sinned and done what is evil in your sight, so that you may be justified in your words and blameless in your judgment.

David knew that if he was ever going to live free, he had to face his failures. When he finally got honest about his sin, only then was he able to ask for God's grace.

You won't take medicine for a disease you refuse to believe you have. You will never accept the help of a Savior if you don't believe you need to be saved. You won't pursue the Great Physician until you realize that you have a great sickness. You will never appreciate how far Jesus came to get you until you are willing to admit how far you ran away. If you don't understand how messed up the problem is, you will never have the motivation to passionately praise God for bringing about his beautiful solution in Christ.

Christians are not supposed to be blindly idealistic or pessimistic, but we are to be realistic. All is not okay. Everything does not turn out for the best when Jesus is not invited into our lives. Hell is a real place. Pain exists. Great opportunities really can be thrown away. People actually do miss out on God's good plan for their lives when they reject God's ways.

The world and our own hearts are far worse off without Jesus than we are sometimes willing to admit. The gospel is only good news if there really is bad news in this world.

Those Who Know They've Been Forgiven Much Love Much

In Luke 7:36-50, there is an account of Jesus teaching the same transformative lesson David is expressing in the beginning of Psalm 51. Jesus explains that those who are honest about their own sin are the ones who end up loving him the most.

As the story unfolds, Jesus is invited to Simon the Pharisee's house for dinner. As Jesus was reclining at the table, the text says that "a woman who had lived a sinful life" (Luke 7:37 NIV) came and knelt at Jesus' feet. As she knelt behind him, it says she was "weeping." Not crying, not sad, but weeping. Imagine the type of wailing where you can barely catch your breath. This passage goes on to say that she uses the massive amount of tears she is producing to wash Jesus' feet. She then dries his feet clean with her hair, kissed them, and poured perfume on them (Luke 7:38).

Of course Simon the Pharisee disapproved of this because Jesus was allowing a sinful woman to touch him, something the Jewish Law forbid. Let's pick up the story in Luke 7:40 (NLT):

> Then Jesus answered his thoughts. "Simon," he said to the Pharisee, "I have something to say to you."
>
> "Go ahead, Teacher," Simon replied.

[41] Then Jesus told him this story: "A man loaned money to two people—500 pieces of silver to one and 50 pieces to the other. [42] But neither of them could repay him, so he kindly forgave them both, canceling their debts. Who do you suppose loved him more after that?"

[43] Simon answered, "I suppose the one for whom he canceled the larger debt."

"That's right," Jesus said. [44] Then he turned to the woman and said to Simon, "Look at this woman kneeling here. When I entered your home, you didn't offer me water to wash the dust from my feet, but she has washed them with her tears and wiped them with her hair. [45] You didn't greet me with a kiss, but from the time I first came in, she has not stopped kissing my feet. [46] You neglected the courtesy of olive oil to anoint my head, but she has anointed my feet with rare perfume.

[47] "I tell you, her sins—and they are many—have been forgiven, so she has shown me much love. But a person who is forgiven little shows only little love."

The woman recognized her sin, was honest, repented, and then had a great affection for Jesus because he forgave her. She had the motivation and the passion to love Jesus so extravagantly because she knew he was the only one who could give her the extravagant gift she sought – the forgiveness of her many sins.

The Pharisee, on the other hand, refused to admit his own sinfulness, thus he refused to believe he needed anything from Jesus. He didn't seek the good news because he refused to believe the bad news. He showed no great love for Jesus because he saw no great need for Jesus. He didn't even show him customary love. No water to wash Jesus' feet, no kiss to greet him, no oil for his head. These things were customary for a host to give his guest. But the Pharisee thought he didn't need forgiveness, therefore he loved little.

David knew that God had forgiven him much, "For he knew his transgressions and his sin was always before him" (Psalm 51:3). David loved God much because he knew God had forgiven him much.

But all this makes you wonder, why did the woman come to Jesus weeping at all? You'd think she would be asking for forgiveness from the people in her personal life she directly sinned against. Did she sin directly against Jesus? Did she even know Jesus before this event? Perhaps she just knew what we all must come to know: All of our sin is ultimately against God.

Sexual Sin Is Against God

Psalm 51:4, "Against you, you only, have I sinned and done what is evil in your sight, so that you may be justified in your words and blameless in your judgment."

David sinned against Uriah, Bathsheba, his men, and all of Israel. And yet in Psalm 51:4 he states, "Against you, you only have I sinned and done what is evil in your sight?"

All sin is ultimately against God. To understand this, we need to know what sin really is. The literal translation of the word "sin" means to "miss the mark." This phrase was used to describe an arrow missing its intended target. What is the intended target that humans are supposed to be aiming at? Answer: glorifying God.

So what is the glory of God? When the invisible attributes of God are made visible, God calls this glory. Therefore to glorify God means to reveal God, to bear his image. This is why Jesus glorifies God the most because he visibly reveals the most about God (Colossians 1:15).

Man was made in the image of God (Genesis 1:27), therefore man was made for the glory of God (Isaiah 43:7). Romans 3:23 states, "for all have sinned and fall short of the glory of God." You'd think this verse would say "all have sinned and fall short of obedience." Sin is not merely a lack of obedience. Sin is missing the mark of glorifying God.

God didn't just make random laws. His commands are a reflection of himself. God commands us to be holy, to be loving, and to be righteous because these are qualities he possesses. By giving us laws, it was as if he was giving us a script on how to imitate him. When we obey God's laws (following the script), we reflect God, thus glorifying him. When we disobey God's laws (not following the script) we are not glorifying God because we are not reflecting his image.

Sexual sin is a personal offense against God because it is not a reflection of God's character. For example: To commit adultery is to conceal rather than reveal the faithfulness of

God. To masturbate is to conceal rather than reveal the selflessness of God. To lust after porn is to conceal rather than reveal the purity of God. To indulge in impure thoughts is to conceal rather than reveal the inner righteousness of God.

All sin, including sexual sin, is ultimately "only against God" because only God is the one we are to be reflecting and glorifying. Of course our sin is against other people too (Matthew 18:15-20). But you can't sin against another person without sinning against God. If you error against a person in such a way where God is not disobeyed, it's called a mistake, not a sin. What makes sin "sin" is when we disobey God, concealing rather than revealing his image, thus "falling short of the glory of God" (Romans 3:23).

If You Desire to Overcome Sexual Temptation, You Have To Do It For God

Only when we see our sin as a personal offense against God will we see it as a serious problem we must reckon with. People will always sin against us, and in our own sinfulness we will want to pay them back. So often our sexual sin is in response to personal relationships we have with other people. If you are mad at your spouse, your fiancé, or your girlfriend, suddenly porn websites seem a lot more attractive. If you are single and you are mad about it, lonely, or lustful for a girl in your life you can't have, internally you will find the false justification to sin sexually.

God is the only one who will never give us a reason to sin against him. If you are trying to remain pure for any other reason other than to please God, that reason will eventually let you down and you will turn back to your sexual sin. People will always let us down, no matter how much they love us. God never will.

Since all sin is against God, he is the only one who is truly able to pardon us from the penalty of our sins. Jesus could die on the cross and redeem all people who receive his grace because Jesus is God, all sin is against God, and therefore God alone has the legal right to do such a supreme act.

When you are so in love with God and you realize that all sin is ultimately a personal offense against him, this vastly increases your chances of resisting sexual temptation

Going Deeper

1. How does knowing your sexual sin is actually against God help you overcome sexual temptation?

2. What's the difference between a mistake and a sin?

3. Why did the sinful woman in Luke 7:36-50 love Jesus so passionately while the Pharisee loved Jesus so little?

4. We all struggle at times to love Jesus as passionately as we would hope. What might some causes be of our lack of passion for pursuing Jesus?

5. In 2 Samuel 12:9, Nathan, who represents the word of God, says to David, "Why have you despised the word of the LORD, to do what is evil in his sight?" How does spending time in

God's word help us hold onto the truth, resist temptation, and realize that everything revolves around God, including our sin?

6. What similarities do you see between Acts 9:4 and Psalm 51:4?

7. How can the death of one man, Jesus, wash away all the sins of those who receive God's grace?

8. What reasons do you want to overcome sexual sin? While these reasons may be good, do you think these reasons will always motivate you? Why or why not?

9. What is your general understanding of the glory of God? How would you define it? How can Christians glorify God?

10. How does sex between a man and woman glorify (reflect) God? Why does sexual sin not glorify God?

Chapter 4: Understanding Our Real Problem (And How It Relates to Porn)

Psalm 51:5-6
Behold, I was brought forth in iniquity, and in sin did my mother conceive me. ⁶ Behold, you delight in truth in the inward being, and you teach me wisdom in the secret heart.

So when David popped out of the womb and the doctor slapped his butt to get him to cry, did David slap him back? Did David start sassing off to his mom and dad, "Jeeze dad, you're wearing that outfit on my first birthday. And mom, what took you so long. Couldn't you have pushed a little faster?" When Psalm 51:5 says that David was sinful from birth, does it mean David sinned at birth?

Obviously Psalm 51:5 means that David was born with a sinful nature, like all of us. He didn't sin and then become a sinner. David eventually sinned because he already was a sinner from the moment of his conception. Runners run, writers write, teachers teach, and sinners sin.

Theologically this is called "original sin." Our first parents (Adam and Eve) sinned. They passed that sin on to the children they conceived, and their kids passed on the sin, until finally their sin can be traced all the way to our sinful nature. It's not popular to preach in our current day and age, but each and every one of us was born with a flawed, sinful human condition.

Jesus compared humans to trees producing fruit, "So, every healthy tree bears good fruit, but the diseased tree bears bad fruit" (Matthew 7:17). He explained further in Mark 7:21-23, "For from within, out of the heart of man, come evil thoughts, sexual immorality, theft, murder, adultery, coveting, wickedness, deceit, sensuality, envy, slander, pride, foolishness. All these evil things come from within, and they defile a person."

Is it any wonder that if our wicked hearts are the problem (Jeremiah 17:9) Jesus has to give us a new heart (Ezekiel 36:26)? If we were born in sin, is it a surprise that we must be born again (John 3:3)? If our old nature is the issue, Jesus knows the solution is to give us a new nature rooted in him (2 Corinthians 5:17).

Suddenly Jesus coming to earth the way he did makes a lot more sense. He had to be born through the Holy Spirit's inception and delivered through a virgin birth so he wouldn't be born with human's sinful nature inherited by our first parent's, Adam and Eve.

To Find the Right Cure, You Have to Rightly Diagnose the Disease

Psalm 51:5, "Behold, I was brought forth in iniquity, and in sin did my mother conceive me."

David was willing to admit what our human nature hates to admit: Apart from Christ, we are flawed at the core. People don't like to hear that they are the problem. They like to hear that they are the solution. They like to hear how special they are, how much potential they have, how much they can accomplish if they really put their mind to it.

Jesus said in John 15:5, "Apart from me, you can do nothing." Do you know what this means in the Greek? It means, "Apart from me, you can do nothing." Jesus isn't speaking figuratively, scholastically, or hyperbolically. If we truly desire to overcome our sexual sin, we must take Jesus' words at face value and submit to this truth.

Porn blockers are good. But I bet most of us have tried that and found another internet device to use, found a way around the blockers, or found a reason to cancel our subscription. You can chuck your computer out the window, cut the cable cord, or only use the internet in public places. But if these external solutions are our only plan to overcome the sin within us, we will keep failing again and again.

External, practical solutions are good. I'm not saying you should stop trying to give yourself every means of success to resist sexual temptation. But external actions like these should be the result of having a healthy heart, because they will never be the cause of a health heart.

When someone's body starts wasting away from cancer, the real problem is not that the body is wasting away. That is a symptom of the real problem. The real problem is that there is a deadly disease inside of the person causing all these painful symptoms. Likewise, our sexual expression of our sin is not the root issue. Our sinful heart apart from Christ is the real problem.

External Sexual Sin Is an Expression of Our Current Internal Condition

God has made humans with the tendency to sexualize their feelings. Intercourse, at its purest form, is the expression of a husband and wife's love sexualized. The love and commitment they have in their hearts towards one another was designed by God to be expressed physically through the joining of one flesh.

Sin corrupts what God originally intended. Sin takes a good thing God made and twists it into something evil. Since sexualizing love is good and glorifying to God in its proper context, sin working through human sexuality uses God's good design in bad ways. God ordained that sex be an expression of the marital love inside a man and woman; sin causes sex to be used to express the evil inside of men and women. The problem is not with the means of expressing what's inside the heart, the problem is with what's inside a sinful heart.

If a wife is feeling distant from her husband because she is holding onto unforgiveness, she is going to withhold her body sexually. If a husband's commitment is wavering because he feels disrespected by his wife and is passive in dealing with this conflict, he often times feels sexually drawn to other women.

Sadly, those who are sexually abused as children are much more likely to become sexual offenders themselves. This occurs because the sinful nature seeks to sexually express the internal feelings. If the internal feelings are feelings of abuse, this person's sinful nature will sinfully express that abuse.

People who were abused did not sin when they were abused, but the sin in them can take the hurt and sexualizes it in sinful ways, causing sinful sexual expressions of inner wounds.

Even if we have not been abused, everyone follows this similar pattern of sexually expressing what they are experiencing inside. Often times, if they are dead and loveless inside, this will be expressed through a complete absence, and even disgust, for all things sexual. If they are angry inside, they may have a tendency to watch and lust over violent porn or fantasies. If they are internally brooding over the disrespect or lack of appreciation they feel, their sexual desires will be drawn towards sins which make them feel respected and valued.

To deal with the sinful sexual expression of our feelings within, we must deal with the feelings and sin within, which will then change the sexual expression.

To Overcome Evil Sexual Expression, Like Porn, You Need Real Love Inside of You

When it comes to indulging in porn, masturbation, adultery, lust, and all other sexual sin, at its most foundational levels, all of this is rooted in a sexualized lack of true, Christ-centered love.

For example: Pornography depicts sexual actions that are degrading, dominating, and dark. No one ever looks at porn with the motive of loving God, their spouse, or the pornstars. People are more tempted to look at porn when they are angry at their spouse, just broke up with their boyfriend or girlfriend, got disrespected at work, and when they have feelings of hatred in their hearts.

Lusting over pornography, specifically, is one of the most prevalent sexual sins of our day. With a verse by verse comparison with 1 Corinthians 13:4-7, we can see how porn is simply an expression of the lack of love within. Sexual sin, like porn use, is the opposite of expressing love:

> "Love is patient, love is kind. It does not envy, it does not boast, it is not proud. It does not dishonor others, it is not self-seeking, it is not easily angered, it keeps no record of wrongs. Love does not delight in evil but rejoices with the truth. It always protects, always trusts, always hopes, always perseveres."

People look at porn when they are impatient to have their desires fulfilled in a godly way, porn is cruel. It is full of envy for things those who watch it don't have, it boast of sexual sin, and there is not one trace of humility in anything pornographic ever made. Porn is very dishonoring to others, it is completely self-seeking, when porn addicts don't get what they want they are quickly angered, and those who watch porn have a long record of evil memories they cannot forget. Porn is a delight in evil and those who watch it rejoice in a form of sex that is based in false, self-centered fantasies. Porn does not protect people, it exploits them. Those who use porn are not trustworthy as this is always a secret, hidden part of their life. Those who use porn feel hopeless, and those who use it are choosing to give up rather than persevere. Porn use really is the opposite of expressing true love.

Porn Use Is the Result of Turning from God

God said in Isaiah 57:8, "Forsaking me, you uncovered your bed, you climbed into it and opened it wide; you made a pact with those whose beds you love, and you looked with lust on their naked bodies." Notice that the end result of forsaking God was looking "with lust on their naked bodies."

Porn use is the result of turning from God. The cycle doesn't start by looking at porn and then becoming less intimate with God. You look at porn because your intimacy with God is already lessening, and then if you don't repent the porn just makes it worse. Sexual sin, like all sin, is merely the thermometer on our personal relationship with the Lord.

We will never be perfect on this side of eternity because our relationship with God will never be perfect on earth. When we are with God for eternity, enjoying our perfect relationship with him, sin will be no more. In the meantime, to overcome sexual sin, we must seek God personally. The more he changes us through our intimacy with him, the more our sexual behavior will change as well.

Sexual sin is the opposite of sexualized love as God intended for a husband and wife. Therefore, the cure to sexual sin is to get the hatred out of your heart and fill it with the love of Christ instead. No one who is full of love for God would ever indulge in porn or other sexual sin. We all know from experience that porn is appealing when we lose focus of God's beauty, his love for us, and our love for him. The cure to sexual sin is to have a real love for God and others, because sexual sin is based in a lack of love brewing in the heart.

The only way we will have this love is if we seek God more than anything else. We must seek to be filled with his Spirit on a daily, moment by moment level. Romans 5:5 explains, ". . . hope does not put us to shame, because God's love has been poured into our hearts through the Holy Spirit who has been given to us." We must, if we are truly children of God, embrace this truth deeply. We must spend our days seeking to live from the new heart God has given us, which is filled with his love, that we might express the love of Christ inside of us.

David was willing to admit the truth, "Not only have I sinned, but apart from God I am a sinner." It's not popular to say, but it's the truth. We are all internally sinful apart from Christ, which we then express externally. Because David is willing to accept his sin, he is willing to admit that he needs a Savior. If we want to overcome sexual sin, we must diagnose the real problem.

The problem is within. Thankfully God desire to give us an inner cure.

God Desires to Give Inner Truth

Psalm 51:6, "Behold, you delight in truth in the inward being, and you teach me wisdom in the secret heart."

David repented by being totally honest about his condition. He was so honest, he was willing to trace his sin back to his own heart. He was not blaming his external circumstances. He just finally confessed his own internal brokenness.

Thankfully David also knew what God truly desired. David knew there was a serious disconnect between what was going on inside of David and what God desired to be inside of David. Psalm 51:6 states, "Behold, you delight in truth in the inward being, and you teach me wisdom in the secret heart."

Because David was willing to truly admit that his "inward being" and "secret heart" were not what God had desired for him, he was then taking another huge step towards redemption. This step will never be taken until we can humbly see the stark contrast between who we are apart from Christ (Psalm 51:5) and what God desires for us in Christ (Psalm 51:6).

There's Only Three Options Regarding the Sinful Nature: Denial, Suicide, or Repentance

When it comes to the sinful nature, the way I see it, there are really only three possible reactions. The first is denial, the second is suicide (either metaphorically or physically), and the third is repentance leading to redemption.

The most common response to the idea of the sinful nature is denial. Rather than accept the horrifying and humbling realization that we ourselves are actually the problem, most humans deny it. One extreme example of this involves Ariel Castro.

If you live in Cleveland, Ohio like me, you won't have to be reminded of who is Ariel Castor. Castro was a local man who abducted three girls between 2002 and 2004 and held them until 2013. He trapped them in his house by making it a dungeon of sorts. He abused them, raped them, intentionally caused them miscarriages, and completely violated them in every way possible.

Finally one of the girls was able to escape and brought the police to rescue the other two. Castro pled guilty to 937 criminal counts of rape, kidnapping, and aggravated murder (in relation to the miscarriages he intentionally caused). He was sentenced to a prison term of life plus 1,000 years without the chance of parole.

If anyone had reason to believe that his heart was wicked and in need of a Savior, this man was him. Once he was caught and finally confronted with his unbelievable sins, instead of really apologizing to his victims, in a rambling statement at his court hearing, he said this, "I am not a monster. I am just sick. I have an addiction, just like an alcoholic has an addiction. I am not a violent person, and I do have value for human life."

When I found this quote in the news, I was currently preaching on Psalm 51. I shared Castro's story as an extreme example of the progressive nature of sexual sin and how once we are confronted with our sinfulness, the temptation is often to deny it. Castro was not asking for forgiveness because he was unwilling to admit his sinful heart. He was willing to admit that he had sinned, just like an alcoholic has sinned. But he was not willing to admit that at the core of who he was, he was a sinner.

I then moved on in my sermon from the Castro example to explain the next option in dealing with the sinful nature. If we don't repent, we will either deny our sinfulness like Castro or commit suicide, physically or metaphorically, through an unending depression stemming from our realization of our wickedness. There is simply no other way to handle the weightiness of feeling your own fundamental, core flaws. If you finally stop your denial and are confronted with the truth of your depravity, but you don't give it all to Jesus through repentance, the only coping mechanisms the human heart has is death.

One month later after I had preached this sermon, Ariel Castro took his bed sheets and hung himself to death in his prison cell. I'm not telling you this to celebrate his death or to boast about my foresight. Castro's actions are simply a very, very extreme example of what happens when sin is left unchecked and you do not repent.

When we finally come face to face with the inner sinfulness that is the root of our sexual sin, we really do only have three options. We can deny our sinfulness to escape its crushing effects. We can commit suicide to try and escape its crushing effects. And thankfully, to the glory of God, we can also repent of our sinfulness through the gospel of Jesus Christ.

The gospel is our only hope.

Going Deeper

1. Do you believe that people are born sinful or that they sin and then become sinful? Why do you believe this?

2. How do solutions look different when we seek to treat the external problems compared to treating the internal problems? Do you agree that an internal problem needs an internal solution?

3. If you struggle with porn, have you tried to use porn blockers or some other external solution? What happened? What are the pros and cons to external solutions to sexual sin?

4. Why do you think porn use is so prevalent these days?

5. What internal feelings and emotions do you have when you are most tempted by sexual sins? Do you see any relationship between your internal feelings and what you are sexually attracted to?

6. What's the difference between godly sorrow and worldly sorrow (2 Corinthians 7:10)?

7. Some people use their sin nature as an excuse, "Well, I can't help myself, I am sinful after all. Thank God for forgiveness." But then they keep sinning and don't truly repent. How does David's realization of his sinful nature help him choose the right road to truly repent?

8. Do you think there is a connection between our passion for Jesus and our personal realization for our own sinfulness apart from Jesus? If we don't think our condition is that bad apart from Christ, do you think this affects our desire to pursue Christ?

9. C.S. Lewis said, "No man knows how bad he is till he has tried very hard to be good." Have you tried very hard to be good in your own power? What was the result?

10. Read about Judas in Matthew 27:1-10. Why did Judas kill himself? How can we avoid denying our sin or being overwhelmed by our sin?

Chapter 5: The Power of the Cross Is Real

Psalm 51:7-9
Purge me with hyssop, and I shall be clean; wash me, and I shall be whiter than snow. [8] Let me hear joy and gladness; let the bones that you have broken rejoice.[9] Hide your face from my sins, and blot out all my iniquities.

In 2006 I was living in Liberia doing missionary work. This West African country was rebuilding from a civil war which lasted over a decade. There was still a somber feeling in the air. It felt like everywhere you went the local people were internally recovering from the atrocities they witnessed firsthand on the very ground we stood.

In the capital city of Monrovia where I was staying, although many of the buildings were still standing, whole walls and huge sections were missing from explosions during the war. As you walked through the streets, the light post no longer worked and they were riddled with bullet holes. The paved roads were a nightmare to drive on. You could disappear within the potholes even though the road crews would be out daily filling them with dirt, the only resource Liberia seemed to have in abundance. As you left the city and headed into the bush, things only got worse.

But there really was a spirit of renewal in the air in those days as well. The civil war was over and the country had elected a new president, Ellen Johnson – the first female Liberian President in their history. Things were starting to look up.

One of the ways some of the people would enjoy the new peace was through basketball. There was a "professional" league based in Monrovia and a few of us were invited to the games. It was there that I met Abraham Freeman. Little did I know how prophetic his name would become to our relationship.

Over the months we became friends, chitchatting at the basketball games, talking about our different cultures, nothing too serious really. He was a regular around the basketball courts, which meant he was one of those guys who seemed to know everyone. He introduced me to one of the personal bodyguards of former Rebel Leader and Liberian President, Charles Taylor. Freeman also introduced me to a variety of local celebrities, like a female Liberian Olympic sprinter. He took a lot of pride in rubbing shoulders with the elites.

All that to say, it was a surprise to me when a few weeks later one of my missionary friends told me he had visited the Monrovian prison and someone there was asking for me, Abraham Freeman. There are not too many white people walking around the streets of Liberia, so when Freeman saw my friend who was leading our prison ministry, Freeman took a chance and asked if he knew me. My friend told me Freeman was asking for me to come and visit. Freeman seemed like a popular guy, and since we were not that close, this was a surprise. I had been to the prisons once before and had wanted to go back, so I packed my backpack and asked a friend to accompany me.

Prisons in Liberia are not the same as they are in America. Through my visits I learned they were so packed that there was literally barely any room for the men to sit down. They fought over the floor space to stretch their legs, there was no electricity, and the only food to eat was wheat bread donated by NATO. Wheat bread, however, is a food source unnatural to the native Liberian people, thus it would cause stomach issues amongst the inmates.

As I talked with Freeman, he confided in me that he spent the last few days awake, leaning against the wall and sitting down when he could, so he would not be raped by the other inmates. This was easily the worse place I have ever visited in my life.

Worst of all, since the political infrastructure was so new and fragile, corruption was rampant in the judicial system. No matter what your crime, basically the only way you would ever get out of a Liberian prison was through waiting years for the judge to get to your case; or you could pay a large fee that the majority of Liberians could never afford. If the judge received the payment, which was basically used as a bribe, he would see your case and release you. If there was no payment made, you sat in jail. You could be a murderer, a person who stole a chicken, or someone who was falsely accused, but these rules applied to everyone.

As I sat with Freeman, taking in all of the atrocities that lay before him now that he was stuck in this circle of corruption, I saw a defeated and hopeless look in his eye. He had changed so much from when I saw him just a few weeks ago. He was now a broken man. He was so lost, tired, and truly had no way of escape. He explained how he could never pay the dept the judge was demanding.

I didn't know if Freeman had done what he had been accused of. Apparently there was a dispute with his female neighbor and when the cops arrived, they ruled against Freeman. I did know that no matter if he was guilty or not, his punishment was not going to fit the crime of which he was accused. I knew he was stuck in a very corrupt system and he could be trapped in this jail for years, or perhaps he would never make it out.

As my visiting time came to a close, I asked, "So how much would it take to get you out of here?"

His eyes rose from the red dirt ground. He paused before answering sheepishly in his broken English, "Sixty USD."

I furrowed my brow in confusion, pondering his answer more thoroughly in my head. It may not seem like much to us, but to Freeman, he owed the judge an insurmountable dept. Freeman, like many Liberians I encountered, simply lived hand-to-mouth. They had no savings, no money, and not much more that the clothes on their body. If they could work for enough food to have a full belly that day, things were good for them.

I clarified with him once again that if I could give him just sixty US dollars, he could give it to the lawyer, who would then give it to the judge, and within days he would be free? Freeman confirmed and I just sat quietly for a few moments, shocked that this man's life was so utterly ruined over just sixty dollars.

"Really Freeman? If I just give you $60 dollars you could go free?"

"Yes, Mark," he confirmed.

With that, I opened up my wallet, took out sixty dollars cash, and handed it to Freeman. He was speechless, mouth opened, and frozen in shock.

We are all like Freeman in that we all owe the Judge a dept we can never pay back. We might have just lusted in our minds, or we may have committed adultery and murder like David, but we all are at the mercy of the Judge. Unlike in Liberia, in God's case, this is just. Someone must pay for what we did.

Jesus Christ paid the dept for the whole world with his death on the cross. And praise God he did, because without the cross, none of us could escape the bondage we have been entangled in through our sexual sins.

To Overcome Sexual Sin, You Must Have Confidence in the Cross

Psalm 51:7,"Purge me with hyssop and I shall be clean; wash me, and I shall be whiter than snow."

In Psalm 51:7, David is expressing his confidence in God's power to restore him. One definition of the word "purge" is "to rid someone of an unwanted feeling, memory, or condition, typically giving a sense of a physiological and emotional release." "Purge" is a verb, meaning it is an action that David is requesting God to actually do to him. The NIV translates Psalm 51:7 as, "Cleanse me with the hyssop, and I will be clean; wash me, and I will be whiter than snow."

Now what the heck is this "hyssop" all about? To really appreciate what David is saying, you have to understand the significance of the hyssop plant in the Old Testament. In Exodus 12:22 the hyssop is used at the first Passover to spread the blood around the doorframes. In Leviticus 14:4-7 the hyssop and the blood are used in the ceremonial cleansing of the leper. In Numbers 19:1 it is used for cleansing someone who has touched a dead body. Basically the hyssop was used to transfer the blood of the sacrifice to the sinner.

The hyssop branch, however, shows up in the New Testament as well, right at the crucifixion of Jesus. John 19:28-30 explains:

> "After this, Jesus, knowing that all was now finished, said (to fulfill the Scripture), 'I thirst.' [29] A jar full of sour wine stood there, so they put a sponge full of the sour wine on a hyssop branch and held it to his mouth. [30] When Jesus had received the sour wine, he said, 'It is finished,' and he bowed his head and gave up his spirit."

It's crazy to me how much symbolism is going on here. Jesus is drinking the wine vinegar. Psalm 75:8 states, "For in the hand of the LORD there is a cup with foaming wine, well mixed, and he pours out from it, and all the wicked of the earth shall drain it down to the dregs." Jesus prayed in Matthew 26:42

(NIV), "My Father, if it is not possible for this cup to be taken away unless I drink it, may your will be done." Therefore it's safe to conclude that the cup of sour wine Jesus drinks at the crucifixion is symbolizing the cup of God's wrath which we all deserve to drink because of our sins. The cup could be taken away from Jesus even if he didn't drink it. But the cup of God's wrath could not be taken away from us unless Jesus drank it on our behalf.

Notice, however, that this wine representing God's wrath was transferred to Jesus on the hyssop branch. The hyssop plant and the wine vinegar are symbolizing the substitutionary death of Jesus on our behalf. He died in our place. He drank the cup of God's wrath that we were supposed to drink. And it was as if God ordained the hyssop branch to show up right at the crucifixion to remind everyone who was watching that all those symbolic rituals in the Old Testament were symbolizing this moment.

It's like he was saying to everyone, "It wasn't the blood of the lamb spread over your doorframe with the hyssop that allowed the angel of death to pass over you when you were leaving Egypt. It wasn't the blood of animals that Moses sprinkled on you with the hyssop that appeased my wrath. It was my Son's blood. I did that. I led you out of Egypt. I paid the price for your rebellion. Look at the hyssop and remember my Son. Look at this Old Testament symbol and now look at the One it was symbolizing."

David may have not fully understood what he was saying, but when he prayed that God would purge him with the hyssop, it was if he was praying that God would release him of the judicial, emotional, physical, and spiritual burden he was under because of his sin. When we see what the hyssop was pointing to, we can read Psalm 51:7 with the understanding, "Cleanse me with Jesus' blood and I will be clean, wash me with his blood, and I will be whiter than snow."

The Cross Purchased More than Forgiveness

Psalm 51:8-9, "Let me hear joy and gladness; let the bones that you have broken rejoice.[9] Hide your face from my sins, and blot out all my iniquities."

David may have not understood the power of Christ's crucifixion, but he did understand the power of God's ability to cleanse and redeem. David knew that his joy would be restored through God's amazing gift of forgiveness. He also knew, however, that God could give him more than forgiveness. David knew that if he was to "hear joy and gladness" once again, his very identity would have to change and God could do this very thing, a fact we will study more in the next chapter.

The cross transforms us not only through forgiveness, but also through crucifying our old sinful nature with Christ. Because Jesus died on the cross and when we put our faith in Christ, our sinful nature dies with him. When you are reborn and transformed into a new creation, the old sinful nature is no longer the real you:

"My old self has been crucified with Christ. It is no longer I who live, but Christ lives in me." (Galatians 2:20 NLT)

"The saying is trustworthy, for: If we have died with him, we will also live with him . . . ." (2 Timothy 2:11)

"We know that our old self was crucified with him in order that the body of sin might be brought to nothing, so that we would no longer be enslaved to sin." (Romans 6:6)

So how does this relate to overcoming sexual temptation? It's pivotal to be forgiven, but how are we going to live free when the sexual temptations come knocking in the future. It's truly an awful existence to be forgiven but left defenseless against your vices, knowing you will just need to be forgiven tomorrow for the same sexual sins confessed today. Because of the cross of Christ, this does not have to be our life anymore.

The power of the cross is real. You are no longer your sinful nature (Romans 7:20). At the moment of your conversion when you put your faith in Jesus and received his grace, you really did become a new creation in Christ. Your sinful nature, however, still remains in your body. The transforming truth of the cross is that though your sinful nature still remains in your body, the true you in Christ is no longer your sinful nature. Those desires you feel for sexual sin, those are not the real you! That's your sinful nature.

That's all well and good, but none of this will actually affect your life until you start believing it deeply.

What You Do Is a Reflection of What You Believe

To overcome sexual sin, we must understand that what we do is a reflection of what we believe about our identity. The cross of Christ not only wipes away your sin, it crucifies your sinful nature.

To explain this idea theologically, you are "positionally" completely righteous, pure, and justified in Christ (1 Corinthians 1:30). Justification is the legal transaction of God who puts the qualities of Christ onto you. When God looks at Christians, he sees the perfections of Christ. He doesn't just look at us this way to be kind, like a naive parent who thinks there little devil is an angel. God always sees the absolute truth. The power of the cross is real.

We all know, however, we don't live a perfect life once we become a Christian. While all Christians are objectively and positionally fully justified in Christ, we are all also being sanctified. The process of sanctification is where you learn to live out who you already are in Christ. This is where the rubber meets the road. And the way sanctification happens is through active faith in your justification.

Justification is something that is done to you; sanctification requires your active participation. When you are justified, God puts Christ's righteousness on you. Sanctification occurs when you participate with the Holy Spirit's leading and you start to live out the righteousness God has given you. The more deeply you believe and trust who you truly are in Christ, the more this will manifest in your day-to-day life. The more you believe in God's justification of you, the more you will experience his sanctification in you.

When you feel the desire to look at pornography or masturbate, you will only overcome these temptations if your beliefs trump your feelings. You must believe that your old-self is crucified with Christ, which means the sinful desires you feel in your body are not the true desires of your new heart. Romans 6:10-12 explains:

> "For the death [Jesus] died he died to sin, once for all, but the life he lives he lives to God. [11] So you also must consider yourselves dead to sin and alive to God in Christ Jesus. [12] Let not sin therefore reign in your mortal body, to make you obey its passions."

Romans 6:10 starts with facts and then in Romans 6:11 Paul instructs us to "consider yourselves dead to sin and alive to God in Christ Jesus." Romans 6:11 in the NIV says you are to "count yourself dead to sin." The KJV says to "reckon ye also yourselves to be dead indeed unto sin." To "consider," to "count," and to "reckon" on something is to put your full trust in it. It's one thing to believe, it's another thing to trust. It's one thing to own an un-cashed check. You own the money, but it's just an objective reality, not a subjective experience of holding the dollars in your hands and spending them. Reckoning on God's truth about your identity in Christ is like cashing the check and using the money.

Subjective feelings follow your beliefs about objective reality. Objectively, you are dead to sin, but subjectively you don't feel dead to sin. In these moments your active faith in biblical facts must reign in your mind and heart. When you relentlessly cling to the truth of Scripture, believing deeply within you that the cross of Christ has really made you someone different than your sinful nature, only then will you have the power to overcome sexual temptation. Freedom starts with clinging to biblical facts:

> "Set your minds on things that are above, not on things that are on earth. [3] For you have died, and your life is hidden with Christ in God." (Colossians 3:2-3)

Notice that "you have died, and your life is hidden with Christ in God." That's a fact. Therefore you must "set your minds on things above, not on things that are on earth." Our actions must flow out of our beliefs of biblical facts. The truth is that you died to sin, but you won't experience this until you set your mind to live in reality. If your mind and beliefs are rooted in your feelings and not God's facts about you, you're dead.

> "Since you have heard about Jesus and have learned the truth that comes from him, [22] throw off your old sinful nature and your former way of life, which is corrupted by lust and deception. [23] Instead, let the Spirit renew your thoughts and attitudes. [24] Put on your new nature, created to be like God—truly righteous and holy." (Ephesians 4:21-24 NLT)

Since "you have learned the truth" (facts), now you must intentionally "throw off your old sinful nature and your former way of life" and "put on your new nature, created to be like God – truly righteous and holy." When you believe with your whole heart that you now hate sin and love God, sexual sin loses its grip on you.

"For freedom Christ has set us free; stand firm therefore, and do not submit again to a yoke of slavery." (Galatians 5:1)

Notice that "Christ has set us free." This phrase is a past tense fact. The rest of Galatians 5:1 explains that we still need to actively "stand firm" in that freedom so we will not live as though we are still in slavery. Because Christ really has already set you free, now you must actively choose to walk in that freedom. Because you are justified, now you have the power to be sanctified.

In Psalm 51:7-9, David is expressing his supreme belief that if God changes him, he really will be changed. Freedom from sexual sin starts when you know the facts about your identity in Christ and actively believe them.

The more deeply you believe and truly trust in the power of the cross, the more deeply this will translate into righteous living.

Going Deeper

1. When you think about Jesus' crucifixion, what benefits do you associate with this?

2. What is justification and sanctification? How do these two terms relate to one another?

3. Do you think there is a difference between belief and trust? How is believing you are a new creation in Christ different than actively trusting this?

4. How does your thought life relate to your actions?

5. What are ways you can assure your thought life is healthy and rooted in biblical facts rather than controlled by your human emotions?

6. Do you believe you have a choice to think about certain things and avoid thinking about other things? In other words, do you believe you can control your mind or does it just control you?

7. Satan often tries to get us to doubt our transformation, "If you were really changed, then why are you still struggling with porn, masturbation, and lust?" What is the biblical answer to this lie? If we really are a new creation in Christ, why do we still sin?

8. Read Romans 7:13-25. Summarize these verses in your own words.

9. Even though the true you is no longer your sinful nature, why is it still absolutely necessary to take responsibility for your sins, confess them to God, and repent? If our sinful nature is responsible for our sins, why are we still to blame?

10. List a handful of Bible verses that proclaim the truth about your real identity in Christ. Challenger yourself to memorize some of these so you are ready to believe biblical facts rather than sinful temptations, urges, and feelings.

Chapter 6: The Power of the Resurrection Is Real

Psalm 51:10
Create in me a clean heart, O God, and renew a right spirit within me.

The American Church has gotten the issue of purity backwards. The idea is presented to youth groups across the country that it is utterly crucial for them to "remain pure." When they are virgins, they have their purity. If they have premarital sex, however, they will lose their purity.

While there are certainly worse things you could tell a teenager, this logic simply does not translate to our spiritual reality explained in the Bible. The Bible explains that if you truly are pure, then your actions will be pure. The fact that people "lose their purity" shows that they were never truly and spiritually pure to begin with.

Our actions are a reflection of who we are and what we believe about our self. A good tree produces good fruit, and a bad tree produces bad fruit (Matthew 7:17). Likewise, a pure human sexuality produces pure actions and an impure human sexuality produces impure actions.

Since we were all born spiritually impure, spiritual purity is not something to be lost. Purity is something that can only be given to us through Jesus Christ. You can't lose your spiritual purity because you were never spiritually pure to begin with. If you were pure you would never have done those impure things. The fruit reflects the tree.

This is one of the biggest lies the American Church has fed our young people, specifically our young ladies. Telling them they have a purity they can lose is not only unhelpful in keeping young people from sexual sin, it also only magnifies their shame when they do sin. They should feel guilty if they commit sexual sin, but often times they feel completely hopeless because they believe they are now permanently damaged goods. They were validated through their own abstinence rather than through Christ. When their abstinence is gone, their whole identity is then lost. If Christ was their identity to begin with, none of this would have happened.

We should definitely teach our young people to abstain from sexual sin, but we should explain that they should do so because they are seeking to honor Christ as they live from the purity he has given them, not so they can earn their own purity through their works (or lack of external sin). We should warn them of the consequences of sexual sin, but we should also warn them of the consequences of thinking they are pure without Christ. When all we are teaching them is to keep something they never had to begin with, they are doomed to fail. Purity is given by Christ. You can't lose what you never had.

The idea that you are born pure and then you can lose your purity is also dangerous because those who do not struggle with sexual sin as much as others think they really do have a purity of their own. Ironically, people who think they are pure because they did practice abstinence are probably the least pure of them all because they are most likely relying on their own works rather than on God's grace. Again, we should commend people's choice to practice abstinence, but we should not confuse them by teaching that they are pure because of their own choices rather than God's mercy. In Jesus' warning to the Pharisees he explained this point further:

> "First clean the inside of the cup and the plate, that the outside also may be clean. Woe to you, scribes and Pharisees, hypocrites! For you are like whitewashed tombs, which outwardly appear beautiful, but within are full of dead people's bones and all uncleanness. So you also outwardly appear righteous to others, but within you are full of hypocrisy and lawlessness" (Matthew 23:26-28)

We must apply this truth to our sexuality. We must seek the purity only Christ can give on the inside so that our external actions will also be clean.

The side effects of the false notion that you are born with a purity you must seek to keep are truly frightening. Not only will those clinging to a purity they don't rely posses be prone to spiritual pride, they will also be prone to struggling with guilt when their own righteousness inevitably lets them down.

Even if you have been taught that you are pure because you don't engage in sexual sin, internally you will know you are not what you are pretending to be. I have witnessed firsthand how prevalent this is among young women who have grown up in the church. They get exalted because of their abstinence, but internally they feel ashamed and guilty because they know they are not as pure as people think they are.

The Gospel Is Not Just the Cross, But the Resurrection Too

Psalm 51:10, "Create in me a clean heart, O God, and renew a right spirit within me."

The power of the gospel starts with the cross but it also includes the resurrection (1 Corinthians 15:1-4). The cross accomplishes our forgiveness and the crucifixion of our sinful nature. The resurrection, however, accomplishes for us a new life.

Not only did we die with Christ, but we were also raised and transformed with Christ as well. As we discussed in chapter 5, this means that because of the cross, the sinful urges we feel are no longer the true us. But now because of Jesus' resurrection, we can also have good urges and desires stemming from our good, new hearts.

David knows that he not only needs to be cleansed from his old desires. He also needs new desires. Therefore he prays, "Create in me a pure heart, O God, and renew a steadfast spirit within me" (Psalm 51:10 NIV). He knows that only out of a pure heart will he produce pure actions.

In Ezekiel 36:26-27 (NLT), God made an awesome promise fulfilled through the resurrection of Jesus Christ and the baptism of the Holy Spirit, "And I will give you a new heart, and I will put a new spirit in you. I will take out your stony, stubborn heart and give you a tender, responsive heart. And I will put my Spirit in you so that you will follow my decrees and be careful to obey my regulations."

David prays for a pure heart and a responsive spirit so he will be able to live a new life. One of my favorite Bible verses about our new life in Christ is Romans 6:4, "We were therefore buried with him through baptism into death in order that, just as Christ was raised from the dead through the glory of the Father, we too may live a new life."

The Greek words used in Romans 6:4 that are translated "new life" are "kainotes" for "new" and "zoe" for "life." Kainotes means "newness of spirit." This is not the type of "new" like when I get a new pair of shoes, which in a year from now will no longer be new. This word denotes that the whole substance is now different. What you were is no longer even the same material as what you are now. Kainotes is that which replaces the obsolete with something that is better, superior, or more advanced.

For example, compared to the typewriter the computer is a new way to print words. Email is a new form of sending information compared to mailing a letter through the post office. Kainotes means different in substance, not chronological order. The computer has been around for awhile now, so it's not new in that sense, but compared to the typewriter, it's different, better, and "new."

For the word "life" Paul used the Greek word "zoe" rather than the word "bios." Bios refers to the type of life that is observable on the outside which you can record. It's where we get our English word for "biography." Zoe however refers to a metaphysical life, a life force that animates a living being.

Therefore "new life" in Romans 6:4, "kainotes zoe," does not mean a fresh start, a new chapter in your biography, or a second chance. It means you have a new name written in an entirely different book. You are not a better version of the former you. You are now a totally new and different person. You are not born a second time, you are "born again" as a different person. You have a new heart and a new spirit. You're of a different substance now, unrelated to your sinful nature. Martin Loyd Jones, teaching on Romans 6, helps us apply this theological knowledge in a practical way:

> "Paul never says that sin is dead; what he does say is that we are dead to sin. Sin is still alive in our mortal body; and if we do not realize that and deal with it, it will soon reign in our mortal body. Sin is not eradicated out of us, and it never will be as long as we are in this mortal body. Sin is in our mortal body and it is always striving for mastery and for control in the Christian. It can never dominate over the life of Christ in him, but it is always striving to dominate his body. It may indeed dominate his body for a time, and when it does so, it is what we call "backsliding." Sin is there . . . you always have to remember that, and not allow it to do so."

So what does this mean in relation to sexual temptation? It means your porn problem is not a computer problem. Could you imagine buying a computer, and then trying to return it the next day, "So, what's wrong with this computer that you want to return?" the salesman asks. "Well," you respond, "this one seems to be malfunctioning. It keeps causing me to lust over things I shouldn't?"

If computers were the problem I would be a millionaire because I would hire some guys to make one that didn't tempt people and sell it to all the Christians who are tired of struggling with porn. It's not as if the engineers and programmers are sitting around the office saying things like, "Hey, did you put the porn tempting program on that new model?" Sexual sin was around before the internet. Satan and sexual sin just use the internet; the internet does not use Satan and sexual sin.

If we hope to overcome sexual temptation, we must not only believe that our old self is dead to us, but we must also believe that we are alive in Christ. We reject the old desires while simultaneously embracing the new desires. It's not enough to only resist evil. You must also pursue good. Romans 12:21 says, "Do not be overcome by evil, but overcome evil with good."

When lust is lurking, you have to remember who you really are. You desire purity, you desire to please God, and you desire to live free. You now desire what is good because Christ has raised you from the dead and made you good.

David was a man after God's own heart because God created in him a pure, clean heart (Psalm 51:10). The resurrection of Jesus Christ does the same for us.

What Happens When I Sin? Can I Lose My Newness?

Sin doesn't change God's faithfulness to us or our righteousness in Christ. Sin, however, does change our experience of God and the experience of our righteousness in Christ. You can never lose your salvation but you can lose your personal intimacy with God. You can still be married to your spouse, but you can also choose to move out and live in another town. By a covenant you are married, but in your relationship you are disconnected. The same can be true in our walk with God.

Becoming a new creation in Christ is not a second chance or a clean slate. The amount of chances we have isn't our problem. It wasn't like we messed up by accident and maybe if we could get a "do-over" we might get it right next time. We don't need more chances. We need a sure thing, which is why God didn't give us back our old life but rather gave us a new life all together that can never be tainted in anyway.

When we sin, we must remember that this means we allowed our sinful nature to take over. We are absolutely still responsible. You can't blame your sinful nature for your sexual sin. When our sinful nature produces sin, we still need to actively repent and ask Jesus to forgive us.

To overcome sexual sin, we must also understand that even though we sinned, we are still a new creation in Christ. Just because you are not fully sanctified does not change the fact that you are fully justified. The sin in your body is not the real you. As Paul said, ". . . it is no longer I who do it, but the sin that dwells within me" (Romans 7:20).

You will never overcome sexual temptation if every time you fall to it, you start doubting the power of the resurrection and your new life in Christ. Our Father transfers the holiness of Jesus to us all the time. We are always pure and righteous because of Christ, even after we sin.

The fact that God always transfers the perfections of Christ to Christians is not an excuse to sin more (Romans 6:1-4). This is now the reason that no matter how many times you fail, you can always get back up and live free in Christ.

David never questioned, "God, why didn't you stop me from sinning like this in the first place?" David never thought the solution to his sin should have been God sovereignly preventing him from sinning. When we think we have ultimately blown it, and therefore our only thought is that we wish God would have stopped us in the first place, we are showing that we doubt the power of the gospel.

God could have stopped us from our every sin, but he sent Christ to die on the cross and rise from the dead instead. It's right to have regret over our rebellion. It's right to wish that we never sinned like we did. But we must also believe and trust that the righteousness of Christ transferred to us by grace through faith really is great enough for the guilt we have incurred.

God didn't have to stop us from our sexual sin because the blood of Christ is more than enough to redeem all of our rebellion. To be free from your sexual sin, you must come to grips with this fact: The cross and resurrection are more than enough to redeem us.

You will fail (1 John 1:8-10). But if you consistently live from your new identity in Christ, you will also fail less and less throughout your life. Sanctification from sexual sin is a journey. You will never be sinless on this side of eternity, but you can sin less and less the more deeply you embrace your true identity in Christ, relying on his power and grace.

Going Deeper

1. Jesus did not die and rise from the dead so you could feel sorry about your sin forever. Jesus died and rose so you could be transformed. What does the resurrection of Jesus Christ accomplish for the Christian?

2. Consider Psalm 51:10 in the light of Matthew 15:19. Do you think it is crucial that solutions to sexual sin must address the issues of the heart? Why or Why not?

3. Revisit what sexual sins you specifically desire to resist? How's it going thus far since you started this study? What are you going to pursue in place of what you seek to avoid?

4. Why did God not stop us when we sinned in the past?

5. Compare 2 Samuel 12:15 and 2 Samuel 12:24. What sticks out to you about the different words used in these verses?

6. What were you taught growing up about sexual purity? How did this negatively or positively affect you?

7. If you can't lose your newness in Christ, what can happen to you when you sin? What are the consequences of sexual sin for a Christian?

8. Is the human heart good or bad? (Read Jeremiah 17:9 and Ezekiel 36:26-27)

9. If the newness of Christ can never be taken away from a Christian, does this fact tempt us to sin more? What should be our reaction to learning that Christ's perfections can never be taken away from us? (Read Romans 6:1-4)

10. If someone asked you why you wanted to overcome sexual temptation, how would you answer?

Chapter 7: Purity Is the Result of God's Presence, Not the Cause

Psalm 51:11
Cast me not away from your presence, and take not your Holy Spirit from me.

David entered the presence of God not because of the great things he did in his life. He did amazing things in his life because he was allowed into the presence of God.

As we have discussed, the heart of God was especially affectionate for the man who was later described by the Lord as, "a man after my heart, who will do all my will" (Acts 13:33). Again, a Bible study on the life of David would not reveal a perfect man, but rather a man who failed and sinned in many ways. So the questions must be asked: Why did God love and bless David so much?

There are many answers which could be given that would not be wrong: David was courageous, he was passionate for the Lord, he was obedient to the Lord, he was a worshipper of God, he was repentant when he sinned, he had great character, and he had a zeal for building the Lord a house. But if you had to pick the most fundamental, core reason for why God loved and blessed David so much it would simply be this: Because God chose him.

Greatness Does Not Produce God's Anointing, God's Anointing Produces Greatness

As tempting as it is to idolize the life of David and exalt his exploits, believing that if we just do what David did God will bless us too, there is a great danger in doing so. Why? Because, ultimately, God's favor on David's life was not based on David's actions.

If it was, God's favor would have been lost once David sinned with Bathsheba (2 Samuel 11) or counted the fighting men (2 Samuel 24) or once he did one of the many other things with which God was not pleased (Psalm 32). Ultimately, David and God's relationship is best understood through the lens of grace.

The first real details we get about the life of David (besides his ancestral line in Ruth 4 and an inference in 1 Samuel 13:14) occurs in 1 Samuel 16 where God directs Samuel regarding David, "'Fill your horn with oil, and go. I will send you to Jesse the Bethlehemite, for I have provided for myself a king among his sons.' . . . Then Samuel took the horn of oil and anointed him in the midst of his brothers. And the Spirit of the LORD rushed upon David from that day forward" (1 Samuel 16:1, 13).

David did not provide God with anything. God provided David for himself. God anointed David before David did anything worthy of note. The Spirit of the Lord rushed upon David, and only then did he later kill Goliath, lead military campaigns, write psalms, plan for the building of the temple, and provide the lineage through which Jesus would be born. Thus, throughout his life, David was wise to appeal to God, not his own rights. He always knew he needed God's favor to remain on him. He prayed, "Keep me as the apple of your eye" (Psalm 17:8). David was dependent upon God's character, not his own.

If we want a relationship with God like David, to be blessed by God like David, then we must seek the grace of God that was given to David. Obedience is to be commended and sought after. But sustained obedience is the result of God's favor, not the cause. Above obedience all Christians should seek the underserved favor, blessings, love, and grace of God. David didn't deserve any of the good that he received. It was because of the character and faithfulness of God that he was blessed so abundantly, and the same is true of all Christians. Psalm 89 explains further:

> You have said, "I have made a covenant with my chosen one; I have sworn to David my servant: [4] 'I will establish your offspring forever, and build your throne for all generations. . . I have found David, my servant; with my holy oil I have anointed him, [21] so that my hand shall be established with him; my arm also shall strengthen him." (Psalm 89:3-4, 20-21, emphasis mine)

David's greatness was because of God, not David. Perhaps what truly set David above the rest was that David knew all of this. David knew God was the reason for David's victories and accomplishments.

Examining Your Salvation Is Evidence of Your Salvation

Psalm 51:11, "Cast me not away from your presence, and take not your Holy Spirit from me."

Is it any wonder why David prayed what he did in Psalm 51:11? He knew the reason for his greatness was because God had graciously granted him access to his presence. He knew that he was a great man because God had anointed him greatly with the Holy Spirit.

As we discussed in the previous chapters, we must continue to ask for forgiveness as we grow in sanctification, continuing to sin less and less; but our sin does not taint our justification and the new life within us (only our experience of it). So if we cannot lose our salvation and purity in Christ, why does David pray Psalm 51:11?

First off, it is important to know that there is a difference between being anointed by the Holy Spirit in the Old Testament and having the Holy Spirit live within you as described in the New Testament.

Secondly, it is biblically impossible to lose your salvation. However, what is possible is that you deceive yourself into thinking you are saved when you really are not. The evidence of salvation is not a prayer of salvation. When we are truly saved we will have a conviction of sin, a continual repentance of sin, a fruitful life for Christ, and our faith will endure to the end. We may stumble, but we will not fall from Christ. If we renounce Christ in actions (through unrepentant, continual sin) or words, this shows we were never truly saved to begin with (1 John 2:19).

David was not worried about losing his salvation. He was worried about not having it to start with. All true Christians should go through a season of genuinely questioning their salvation. Their doubt should not be in God's grace, but in their true and genuine faith.

We should not jump to this season of questioning our salvation every time we sin. We should not remain in this season for very long. But we should question our salvation if we are no longer repenting of our sin or if we have grown so callused we just don't care anymore about our rebellion.

If you've never taken a hard look in the mirror and asked yourself if you really believe that Jesus Christ has saved you, that's not healthy. A healthy fear of God will produce a healthy fear of condemnation. There is no condemnation for those who are in Christ Jesus (Romans 8:1), therefore we should examine ourselves to make sure we are truly in Christ Jesus.

You must question the authenticity of your own salvation because no one else has this right or obligation. We each are responsible to examine our own hearts because we can never know anyone's internal condition other than our own. Paul instructs, "Examine yourselves, to see whether you are in the faith. Test yourselves" (2 Corinthians 13:5).

If your repetitive sexual sins have made you question your own salvation, this is a good sign that you truly are saved.

Examining yourself is evidence that the Holy Spirit is really working in you. Those who never examine themselves and never care about their chronic sins should be afraid.

The Bible gives us great comfort that God's grace will absolutely never leave anyone who has received it (Jude 1:24). Far too often, however, the doctrine of eternal security is abused by those who should not feel so secure. While the Bible certainly teaches that there is nothing that can separate us from the love of God (Romans 8:31-39), it also instructs us that if we consistently walk in sin without repenting, something is seriously wrong and we may not be truly saved (1 John 3:8-20).

You Always Fear Losing What You Value the Most

David also prayed Psalm 51:11 because he was expressing what was of the greatest value to him. You always fear losing what you value. This is why mothers get so protective of their children, boyfriends get possessive of their girlfriends, sports players fight to win the game, and why people pleasers do all they can not to embarrass themselves publicly.

Everyone fears losing whatever they see as extremely important. If you wonder what you care about, just ask yourself what you are afraid of losing. This can reveal good things that we love and bad things that we shouldn't love. Are you afraid of losing your spouse to your porn and masturbation addiction? That's a good fear. Or are you afraid of losing the comfort of porn and masturbation if your spouse finds out? That's not so good.

When David fears losing the intimacy he has with God the Holy Spirit, it shows that intimacy with God was David's highest aim.

David was obsessed with the presence of God in his life. He prayed in Psalm 27:4 (NIV), "One thing I ask from the LORD, this only do I seek: that I may dwell in the house of the LORD all the days of my life, to gaze on the beauty of the LORD and to seek him in his temple."

When we fear losing our spouse, telling our accountability partner, or losing our standing at church because of our sexual sins, we are showing that these things rather than God are what are most important to us. You will only honor others in your life and stop sexual sin when God becomes most important to you.

Only when our relationship with God himself is our highest goal will we have the courage and motivation to resist sexual temptation. We should all pray like David did in Psalm 51:11, not because we fear losing our salvation, but because God himself is our highest aim.

Saul's Failure of No Psalms

Have you ever seen a leader fall from a high position? David did. By witnessing what happened to King Saul, David witnessed first had what would happen if God's anointing left him.

1 Samuel 16:1 explains, "The LORD said to Samuel, 'How long will you grieve over Saul, since I have rejected him from being

king over Israel? Fill your horn with oil, and go. I will send you to Jesse the Bethlehemite, for I have provided for myself a king among his sons."

David prayed that God would not remove the Holy Spirit from him because he feared ending up like Saul. 1 Samuel 18:12-14 explains, "Saul was afraid of David because the LORD was with him but had departed from Saul . . . And David had success in all his undertakings, for the LORD was with him."

David and Saul were both anointed to be king of Israel; the Spirit of the Lord came upon them both, enabling them to do great things for the Lord. Why, though, did Saul falter while David flourished? There's so many answers we could give, but God makes it crystal clear for us, "I regret that I have made Saul king, for he has turned back from following me and has not performed my commandments" (1 Samuel 15:11).

Saul got lost in all the power and stopped following God. He forgot the main mission and started idolizing the lesser things. He forsook the Giver of the gifts and started worshipping the gifs themselves.

When Saul disobeyed God and did not utterly destroy the wicked cities and plunder, "Saul said to Samuel, 'I have sinned, for I have transgressed the commandment of the LORD and your words, because I feared the people and obeyed their voice" (1 Samuel 15:24). And then when David started becoming successful and the women started singing a song honoring him, Saul states, "They have ascribed to David ten thousands, and to me they have ascribed thousands, and what more can he have but the kingdom?" (1 Samuel 18:8).

Saul lost sight of God and started seeking the fame that God gave him. He was supposed to use his position to honor and glorify the Lord, not himself. The main difference between Saul and David was that David did not lose his First Love.

When all the success and fame started coming David's way, his main desire was still to please the Lord. When he sinned he eventually always came to his senses. He always repented and sought the Lord above all other things. He was not crushed by the weight of blessings nor by the removal of blessings when God disciplined him. He sought the Giver over the gifts. Because he sought God over the blessings, unlike Saul, despite his many failures, David remained blessed.

I find it interesting that it was David, not Saul, who wrote the majority of the Psalms. Passionate love poems came out of the heart of David, not Saul; and it was on David, not Saul, whom God lavished such favor.

So with every degree of success and blessing God gives us, may our journals and hearts multiply lines of praise and adoration for God alone. If we want to be like David and not Saul, then God and not the external blessings must hold the affections of our hearts.

In the midst of being king over a nation, living in a palace, and having people idolize him for all his great feats, David wrote, "I say to the LORD, 'You are my Lord; I have no good apart from you'" (Psalm 16:2). Notice David made it personal. He said to "the Lord" that God was "my Lord." Our personal relationship with God must be our highest aim.

Saul's failure was that he never had the heart of a worshipper, a psalmist, and rather wanted to be worshipped himself. He did not want to write songs about God, he wanted the songs to be written about him. May our hearts be different so we, like David, will be men and women after God's own heart.

Going Deeper

1. Do you believe you can lose your salvation? Why or why not?

2. Why do you think King David prayed Psalm 51:11?

3. Read Galatians 5:16-26. How does this passage of Scripture help us overcome sexual temptation?

4. What differences do you see between King Saul and King David?

5. How does praising God, like David did in the Book of Psalms, help us live pure?

6. Read Romans 13:13-14. How does being in the presence of God relate to our ability to fight temptation?

7. Read Psalm 101:1-4. What was one of David's techniques of avoiding sin?

8. Read Psalm 16. What jumps out to you about this passage of Scripture?

9. What do you fear losing if you continue to live in sexual sin?

10. Do you see the benefits of keeping a prayer journal? David wrote prayers to God about what was on his heart. Consider challenging yourself to write out prayers to the Lord like David. What prayer commitment do you feel led to make?

Chapter 8: Power Through Rest

Psalm 51:12
Restore to me the joy of your salvation, and uphold me with a
willing spirit.

In Jesus' time on earth, one of his main battles with the
Pharisees revolved around the Sabbath. The Jews were
governed by the laws of the Torah, and there it explicitly
states not to work on the Sabbath.

The Pharisees turned God's law into a list of "do's and don'ts"
by which one could attain a right standing with God. From the
beginning, however, God had a much different purpose for his
commands. Jesus said, "Do not think that I have come to
abolish the Law or the Prophets; I have not come to abolish
them but to fulfill them. . . . For I tell you that unless your
righteousness surpasses that of the Pharisees and the
teachers of the law, you will certainly not enter the kingdom
of heaven" (Matthew 5:17, 20).

Everything in the Old Testament finds its fulfillment in Jesus
Christ. Just as Abraham was counted righteous because he
believed God (Romans 4:3), everyone else before the time of
Christ was to obey the law of God not to earn their salvation,
but to express their belief in God through their obedience.
Those who sought to follow God's commands before Christ
came were actually expressing their faith in Christ, who was
the one these commands were pointing to (Romans 3:19-31,
John 5:39).

Therefore, when it comes to the Sabbath, the Pharisees were completely missing the point as they did with all of God's commandments. They thought by obeying the commandments, such as resting on the seventh day, they were earning their own righteousness with God. Jesus sought to correct this faulty thinking, showing us that we are to obey his commandments as a way of expressing faith in God.

When we disobey the law, the law shows us we are not living from faith in God (Romans 3:20). When we are obeying the law, it shows us that we are living out of God's righteousness he has freely given us when we put our faith in him, "We know that we have come to know him if we keep his commands" (1 John 2:3). We are saved by grace and not my works (Ephesians 2:8-9), but when we receive grace we will complete the good works God has prepared in advance for us to do (Ephesians 2:10).

Perhaps this is one of the reasons why the New Testament Church started practicing the Lord's Day (Sunday) which is on the first day of the week rather than the Sabbath (Saturday) which was on the seventh day of the week. The old way instructed people to work all week and then rest. They were to imitate God who earned his rest during the creation account by working six days and then resting on the seventh.

Now believers rest on the first day of the week. Perhaps God has ordained it this way as a symbolic recognition that we can never earn our own rest. Rather, in the new covenant we must now seek to work from the rest God freely gives us. We rest on the first day of the week to prepare for the work rather than resting on the seventh day as though we earned our own rest because we did work.

Jesus was raised from the dead on the first day of the week (Sunday). Therefore as redeemed people who live from the power of the resurrection, it makes symbolic sense to practice the spirit of the Sabbath on Sunday. Before Christ came, everyone thought that we had to earn our rest through works. Now God has shown us we must produce good works out of the rest he has freely given us in Christ Jesus.

The old way was to work and then rest, but the new way is to rest and then work. With Jesus came a cosmic shift in our relationship to God.

A Lack of Joy and Rest Leads to Rebellion

Psalm 51:12, "Restore to me the joy of your salvation . . . ."

David knew that he could never work hard enough to be restored. He knew, rather, that if he was to work for God again, he would need God to first restore him. Notice the root word to "restore" is "rest."

To resist sexual temptation, we cannot underestimate the importance of being rested in the Lord. More often than not, one of the main triggers for sexual sin is being exhausted. Let's look again at the details leading up to David's sexual sin with Bathsheba:

> In the spring of the year, the time when kings go out to battle, David sent Joab, and his servants with him, and

all Israel. And they ravaged the Ammonites and besieged Rabbah. But David remained at Jerusalem.

"It happened, late one afternoon, when David arose from his couch and was walking on the roof of the king's house, that he saw from the roof a woman bathing; and the woman was very beautiful. And David sent and inquired about the woman. (2 Samuel 11:1-3)

David was clearly tired. He was supposed to be at war, but apparently he felt the need to rest at home instead. It also specifically states "David arose from his couch." He was lounging around, clearly whipped and seeking comfort in reprieve. Lastly, the text makes it clear that it all started "late one afternoon."

Most of us can relate to this scene before David's sexual failure. How many times have we fallen to sexual temptation when we were tired, when we were just laying around on the couch, and late at night when our internal defenses were weakened from a long day at work?

David knows that if he is to change his behavior, he needs restoration and joy in the Lord. He knows that fighting God's battles is exhausting, and the fight never brings the rest and joy his heart needs. He understands that he's gotten the whole thing backwards. Rather than fighting for rest and joy, he knows he needs to fight from his rest and joy given by God's grace.

Overcoming Temptation Through Joy in the Lord

The Bible is full of instructions on how to resist and fight Satan. Perhaps the best place to look, however, is in Matthew 4:1-11 where Jesus prevails against the devil's temptations in the wilderness.

As we study Jesus' victory over temptation, it's clear that Satan's greatest attacks most often do not come in the form of pain and suffering. The devil's greatest attacks come in the form of sinful pleasures. Satan uses suffering not as an end goal but as an opportunity to tempt Christians with sinful pleasure. He desires to get people to avoid pain now through sinful means so they will forsake God and suffer for eternity later.

Notice the timing of when Satan came against Jesus, "And after fasting forty days and forty nights, he was hungry" (Matthew 4:2). Jesus was beaten up, tired, and hungry. Satan didn't cause Jesus' hunger. Satan, however, tried to use those hunger-pains to get Jesus to seek sinful pleasure rather than God.

In all three temptations, Satan worked to get Jesus to take hold of pleasure without any suffering for God. The devil tried to get Jesus to eat some bread immediately (Matthew 4:3), but Jesus knew he would be able to eat bread later. The devil tried to get Jesus to test the Father's saving power now (Matthew 4:5), but Jesus knew the Father would prove his saving power later. The devil tried to get Jesus to take control over the earth now (Matthew 4:9), but Jesus knew the Father would make every kingdom bend the knee to him later.

Again and again, Satan's attack on Jesus was not to make him suffer, but to make him pursue pleasure in sinful ways. Satan wanted Jesus to take for himself what God was going to give him.

At the core of the devil's assault on humans is the temptation to put self above God. "Aren't *you* hungry?" "Don't *you* want the angels to attend to *you*?" "Wouldn't it be nice if *you* had authority over all these earthly kingdoms?" In each of Satan's three temptations, he worked to get Jesus to focus on Jesus.

To better understand how Jesus was able to resist these temptations, let's take a closer look at each of the Scriptures he quoted against the evil one's attacks:

> Matthew 4:4, "It is written 'Man shall not live by bread alone, but by every word that comes from the mouth of God.'"

> Matthew 4:7, "Again it is written, 'You shall not put the Lord your God to the test.'"

> Matthew 4:10, "Be gone, Satan! For it is written, 'You shall worship the Lord your God and him only shall you serve.'"

Satan's goal was to get Jesus' eyes off of God and onto himself. Jesus fought Satan by focusing his attention not on himself but on his Father. Notice in each of the Scriptures Jesus quoted, the emphasis is put back on God. "You shall live by the words from the mouth of *God*. You shall not test *God*.

You shall worship no one but *God*." Satan wants you to focus on *you*. Jesus shows us we must focus on *God*.

As Jesus' death on the cross neared, he prayed in John 12:27-28, "Now is my soul troubled. And what shall I say? 'Father, save me from this hour'? But for this purpose I have come to this hour. Father, glorify your name." Jesus was able to resist the temptations of Satan and endure the sufferings of the cross because his main concern was not with himself but with his Father's glory.

Jesus overcame temptation by looking to a greater reward in God. If we hope to overcome temptation, we must do the same, "And let us run with perseverance the race marked out for us, fixing our eyes on Jesus, the pioneer and perfecter of faith. For the joy set before him he endured the cross, scorning its shame, and sat down at the right hand of the throne of God" (Hebrews 12:1-2, NIV).

Jesus was not a lover of pain. He is a lover of pleasure in God. God is not a prude. He desires for us to have maximum joy, and he knows maximum joy is found within himself. Sin occurs when we lack joy and satisfaction in God. Nobody cheats on their spouse when they are finding great pleasure in their marriage. Infidelity occurs when dissatisfaction arises. The same is always true in our walk with God as well.

Repentance should not only be about running away from the pleasures of sin but also towards the greater pleasures in Christ. Our sin occurred because of our lack of holy joy and satisfaction. If we would have been full of the pleasures of Christ, we would not have gone looking in other places.

Therefore to repent, we must seek to do right where we went wrong. We were wrong to seek pleasure in sinful ways. We must do right not by avoiding pleasure all together, but by seeking a greater pleasure in the right place – God.

Nehemiah 8:10 explains, "For the joy of the LORD is your strength." If we want the power to resist sexual temptation, we must not just try to resist the allures of lust. We must seek something better. We must resist the evil while seeking the good (Romans12:21, James 4:7). We must live like Jesus, who for "the joy set before him he endured the cross."

God's Sovereignty Does Not Take Away Our Free Will, It Sets Our Will Free

Psalm 51:12, ". . . and uphold me with a willing spirit."

If you haven't noticed in Psalm 51:10-12, David is really focusing on the spiritual side of things, "renew a right spirit within me (verse 10) . . . take not your Holy Spirit from me (verse 11) . . . and grant me a willing spirit, to sustain me (verse 12, NIV).

Certainly Psalms 51 is layered with a Hebrew poetic writing style called "parallelism." This is where the poet repeats in different language what he just said to drive home the point. However, something more is going on here.

David is not only focusing on the spiritual side, he is also focusing on God's complete sovereignty over the human spirit. He knows God must renew a right spirit within him. He knows

God alone has the power to anoint his spirit with the Holy Spirit. He knows that only God can give him a willing spirit.

Often times people can feel frozen when they start thinking about the sovereignty of God. The logic goes something like this: If God's will is going to happen no matter what, then my actions and choices really don't matter. If God elects people to salvation, then my evangelistic efforts are worthless. If God is the one who works in me and is the source of all the good I do, then there is really no chance to change my behavior. And if God's grace is given when I sin, why does it matter if I sin?

Jesus said in John 15:5, "Whoever abides in me and I in him, he it is that bears much fruit, for apart from me you can do nothing." While to some this verse gives great comfort, to others it brings great confusion. If I can't do anything without Christ, why I am responsible anyways? People often feel man's free will is somehow voided by God's sovereignty.

The fact that we can do nothing good without Christ does not mean we are called to do nothing. Christ gives us power to act, but we must still choose to live in that power and act. Notice in John 15:5 we are told that we can do nothing without Christ, but we are still left with a specific command we are to do. We are told to "abide" in Christ. This involves active effort.

Jesus had to die on the cross for us, but he still tells us to take up our cross daily (Matthew 16:24). This is an active command, requiring a choice of the will and action from the body. We won't be able to do it if we are not relying on Christ and putting our faith in his truth, but we are called to do these things (with Christ) nonetheless.

His power makes possible our right choices and actions, but we are still responsible to make these right choices and actions. The fact that Jesus is the only power able to cause us to do good is not an excuse for our personal failures. His power is the reason we have no excuse for not doing good.

Philippians 2:12-13 (NLT) states, "Work hard to show the results of your salvation, obeying God with deep reverence and fear. [13] For God is working in you, giving you the desire and the power to do what pleases him."

If you were to read Philippians 2:13 in isolation, you would have a reason to argue that if it is God who works in us to give us both the desire and the power to obey him, then why are we responsible when we don't have good desires and we disobey God? However, when you read Philippians 2:12 and 2:13 together, this logic is turned on its head. God's power in us is the reason we should act rightly, not an excuse to not act rightly. We are told to obey God. Why? "For it is God who works in you . . . ." God's power in us is why God now expects us to obey him.

Unfortunately the emphasis has often become that you don't have to do anything but rely on God, but that's not the emphasis of the Bible. It's not wrong to state how there is nothing we can do without God's power and grace. But to emphasize the "do nothing" part is to emphasize what the Bible does not, thus altering its true meaning. The Bible's emphasis is not on how you don't need to do anything; its emphasis, rather, is on how you can't do anything to be saved in your own power. It still nonetheless requires you to actively obey Jesus Christ's commands, choose to repent of sin, and willfully participate in your own sanctification.

Again the emphasis in the Bible is not that we must sit idly by as we wait on God to do it, but rather that God has already done the impossible for us and therefore we must actively rely on him. Mark 10:26-27 says, "And they were exceedingly astonished, and said to him, 'Then who can be saved?' Jesus looked at them and said, 'With man it is impossible, but not with God. For all things are possible with God.'"

The Bible points out our desperate need for God's power not to give us an excuse to disobey; it tells us to rely on God's power so we know there is now no excuse left not to obey him (Romans 6:1-4).

God's sovereignty does not contradict man's free will. Because of God's sovereign power working in the Christian, we now have a will that is truly free. Before Christ came into your life, you could not disobey the sin living in you. Because of Christ, we now can choose to willfully live free, "For the law of the Spirit of life has set you free in Christ Jesus from the law of sin and death" (Romans 8:2).

Going Deeper

1. Does it feel wrong to you to seek personal joy and pleasure from God? Does this ruin your motives in loving God?

2. Why does King David pray that God would give him a willing spirit? Is God or King David in control of King David's will?

3. Does repentance involve just running away from sin, or does it also include running towards something better? (Romans12:21, James 4:7)

4. Do you feel more vulnerable to sexual temptation when you are tired? What can you do to avoid giving into temptation during these times of exhaustion?

5. How does focusing on yourself hinder your ability to overcome sexual temptation?

6. Do you think it is significant that in each of Jesus' responses to Satan's temptations (Matthew 4:1-11), his answer began with "It is written"? Why or why not?

7. Read Hebrews 12:1-3. What was Jesus' motivation? How should this affect the way we fight temptation?

8. What does it mean when the Bible says "the joy of the Lord is your strength" (Nehemiah 8:10)?

9. How do God's sovereignty and your free will connect? How does God's authority empower our freedom rather than take away our freedom?

10. Rest doesn't just happen. We have to make time to rest. Take a few moments to write down your weekly schedule. Where can you make time to intentionally rest in the Lord?

Chapter 9: Redeemed Transgressors Make the Best Teachers

Psalm 51:13-17
Then I will teach transgressors your ways, and sinners will return to you. Deliver me from bloodguiltiness, O God, O God of my salvation, and my tongue will sing aloud of your righteousness. O Lord, open my lips, and my mouth will declare your praise. For you will not delight in sacrifice, or I would give it; you will not be pleased with a burnt offering. The sacrifices of God are a broken spirit; a broken and contrite heart, O God, you will not despise.

Jacob was a chronic liar. Judah refused to take care of his helpless daughter-in-law, Tamar. Tamar tricked her father-in-law, Judah, to have sex with her. Rahab was a prostitute. Ruth was a Gentile Moabite, a people cursed by God. David, as we know, was an adulterous murderer. Bathsheba married the man who killed her husband. And Solomon followed in his father's footsteps but took their idolatry of women a step further by marrying hundreds of women who turned his heart from God.

What do all of these people have in common? Besides having a shady past, they are all specifically mentioned in the lineage of Jesus (Matthew 1). And these are just a few of the sketchy characters mentioned on this list. Clearly God is making a point by using such broken and rebellious people to bring his Son to earth.

So many times we think our sinful history has disqualified us from a holy, fruitful future. But God uses messed up people because he desires all the glory. David deserved to lose the Holy Spirit. He deserved to always be remembered for his failures. And David deserved to be laughed at when he prayed that he, of all people, would "teach transgressors [God's] ways" and thus because of his help other "sinners will return to [God]."

And yet here we are thousands of years later, studying Psalm 51, proving David was and still is being used by God to instruct and help other sinners like him. God desires to do the same with us.

It's interesting in Matthew 1 to take a closer look at the details shared regarding David and Bathsheba, "David was the father of Solomon, whose mother had been Uriah's wife" (Matthew 1:6). Under the direction of the Holy Spirit, Matthew made sure we all knew the details regarding David, Bathsheba, and Uriah. It's as if God highlights the sinful past as a way of exulting how amazing his grace is through Jesus Christ.

God uses people like David and people like us because God deserves all the glory. If God only used people because they were perfect through their own works, then those perfect people would deserve the praise, not God. God never does this because, for one, there are no perfect people. More than that, however, is the truth that God uses broken people because he desires all the glory.

Our Good Works Are a Result of God's Grace

When David sinned with Bathsheba, he was supposed to be at war (2 Samuel 11:1). Growing up, it was always explained to me that the reason David sinned was because he was not doing what he was supposed to be doing. If he was busy fighting God's battles, he would not have been tempted by Bathsheba's beauty.

Certainly there is some truth to this, but David's motives behind his actions run deeper than his external decisions, as is the case for all of us. A correct theological assessment of David's downfall is not that he sinned with Bathsheba because he was not at war. Rather, he was not at war because his relationship with God was suffering. Sin is progressive, so David's downfall just kept getting worse. He stayed home from his duty as king, then he committed adultery, and then he committed murder. The fact that he was not at war was not the cause of the future sins, it was simply the first symptom of a greater problem.

Sin is a symptom of our weak relationship with God. We may think we have a great, thriving intimacy with our Lord, but our actions are the true thermometer of our spiritual health.

We Are Not Saved By Works, But We Are Saved "For Good Works"

Our usefulness flows from our closeness to God. Our closeness does not flow from our usefulness. You won't get closer to God by doing good. But when you get close to God through his costly grace, he causes you to do good.

Ephesians 2:8-9 has become a favorite passage of Scripture for the modern evangelist, "For by grace you have been saved through faith. And this is not your own doing; it is the gift of God, not a result of works, so that no one may boast." There should of course be an emphasis that we are saved by grace alone. When grace truly saves, though, it is never alone; for it is always accompanied by the good works of those who truly receive it. We are not saved by works, but when we are saved we will naturally produce good works.

Again, it's right for us to emphasize how we can never work hard enough to be saved, forgiven, and redeemed. But it is a crime to not also read Ephesians 2:10 to emphasize the whole picture Scripture seeks to paint, "For we are his workmanship, created in Christ Jesus for good works, which God prepared beforehand, that we should walk in them."

Therefore, it's safe to say that we are saved "by grace," "through faith," and "for good works." Again, we are not saved by works, but we are saved "for good works" done unto God. David emphasizes this point throughout Psalm 51:13-17.

Serve Because You Are Loved. Don't Try To Serve So You Will Be Loved

Psalm 51:13, "Then I will teach transgressors your ways, and sinners will return to you."

Psalm 51:13 is an expression of audacious faith. This is confidence in the power of God. David is guilty of horrible sins, and yet here he is, saying that if God truly changes him, not only will he be free, but he will also be able to teach others how to be free.

The message of Psalm 51:13 would be extremely disturbing if it was found in Psalms 51:1. If David started his prayer of repentance by promising God he would teach other sinners, God would have looked at David with a serious look of concern. As we know, that's far from what David did. Psalm 51:13 starts with the word "Then." Remember in Psalm 51:10-12 David has asked God to transform his heart and grant him a willing spirit. "Then" David proclaims how God can use him to teach other transgressors.

In Psalm 51, David did not start with the future fruit he hopes to produce. He didn't start with his works and actions. He never tried to strike a deal with God based on his deeds. Before he started talking about what he was going to do for God, David started by first dealing with his own need of God. He knew that if God transformed and sanctified his inner being, then his outer life would change as well. Jamming fruit into roots will not make the tree healthy. When the roots are healthy, the tree's fruit will be healthy too (Matthew 7:17).

Psalm 51:13 says a lot about David's willingness to accept God's gift of redemption. Once he receives God's grace, he does not mourn forever over his past mistakes. After an appropriate time of mourning, he then moves on.

To be able to help others with their sexual sins, you have to deal with the shame you feel for your own past. One of the indicators of truly moving on and having faith in God's grace is when you have a desire to help others without feeling like a hypocrite. Your failures do not disqualify you from helping others, only your unforgiven and unrepentant failures do. When you have the faith to believe that God's mercy is more than enough for your lustful past, only then will you feel confident that you are fit to help others where you yourself have struggled.

You don't need a perfect past to help others. God often produces his greatest witnesses by allowing them to personally witness his astounding, lavish grace in their own sinful lives. People who know they were great sinners before they came to Christ (or before they repented of their backsliding) are always the ones with the most passion for him (Luke 7:47). And those who have experienced God's mercy the most are always the best at leading others to do the same.

Love God And People By Proclaiming What God Has Done For You

Psalm 51:14-15, "Deliver me from bloodguiltiness, O God, O God of my salvation, and my tongue will sing aloud of your righteousness. [15]O Lord, open my lips, and my mouth will declare your praise."

There are countless good actions God desires for Christians to produce. Besides loving God, however, the most important action God wants us to produce is to love other people. When asked what the greatest commandment in all of Scripture was, Jesus explained, "You shall love the Lord your God with all your heart and with all your soul and with all your mind and with all your strength.' The second is this: 'You shall love your neighbor as yourself.' There is no other commandment greater than these" (Mark 12:30-31).

One of the greatest ways to love God and other people is to declare what God has done for you. Psalm 40 is strikingly similar to Psalm 51. David proclaimed to the Lord:

> "In sacrifice and offering you have not delighted, but you have given me an open ear. Burnt offering and sin offering you have not required. . . . I have told the glad news of deliverance in the great congregation; behold, I have not restrained my lips, as you know, O LORD. I have not hidden your deliverance within my heart; I have spoken of your faithfulness and your salvation; I have not concealed your steadfast love and your faithfulness from the great congregation." (Psalm 40:6-10)

Once God sets your free, he expects you to tell other people. God saves us because he loves us, but he also saves us for his glory. God wants everyone to worship him. Perhaps if you told others how God has set you free from sexual addiction and temptation, they may seek God's grace as well.

Regardless of the results it may have on other people, when God delivers us, we must "sing aloud of [God's] righteousness. O Lord, open my lips, and my mouth will declare your praise" (Psalm 51:14-15). David knows God must do it for him. But he also knows if God delivers him and opens his mouth, the result will be that he will express this to other people.

Give Others What God Has Given You

Psalm 51:16-17, "For you will not delight in sacrifice, or I would give it; you will not be pleased with a burnt offering. [17]The sacrifices of God are a broken spirit; a broken and contrite heart, O God, you will not despise."

Psalm 51:16-17 reminds us once more that the sacrifices and good works we give to God are not what are making us right with him. Psalm 51:13-17 is driving home the point that we are responsible to do good, to help others as we have been helped, all while embracing the fact that our good works are produced by God's grace and the Holy Spirit working through us.

Towards the end of David's life, when he was dedicating the materials he had saved for the construction of God's temple his son Solomon was to build, David expressed these truths in 1 Chronicles 29:10-20:

> "David praised the LORD in the presence of the whole assembly, saying . . . 'Wealth and honor come from you; you are the ruler of all things. In your hands are strength and power to exalt and give strength to all. Now, our God, we give you thanks, and praise your glorious name.
>
> But who am I, and who are my people, that we should be able to give as generously as this? Everything comes from you, and we have given you only what comes from your hand. . . . LORD our God, all this abundance that we have provided for building you a temple for

your Holy Name comes from your hand, and all of it belongs to you. I know, my God, that you test the heart and are pleased with integrity. All these things I have given willingly and with honest intent. And now I have seen with joy how willingly your people who are here have given to you. LORD, the God of our fathers Abraham, Isaac and Israel, keep these desires and thoughts in the hearts of your people forever, and keep their hearts loyal to you. And give my son Solomon the wholehearted devotion to keep your commands, statutes and decrees and to do everything to build the palatial structure for which I have provided.' Then David said to the whole assembly, 'Praise the LORD your God.' So they all praised the LORD, the God of their fathers . . . ."

It was "before the assembly" that David prayed these profound words. As an old, dying man, you can feel the emotion pouring out of him. He is expressing to those he loves what he learned the hard way as a younger man. Everything good comes from God, including a good heart. Therefore, out of his love for God and gratitude for what his Lord had done for him, he prays that others would grasp this truth as well.

David witnessed how willingly the people loved God, but he also knew God's sovereignty and protection needed to preserve their love for him, so he prayed, "keep these desire and thoughts in the hearts of your people forever, and keep their hearts loyal to you." As we discussed in Chapter 8, God's sovereignty does not violate our free will, it sets our will free.

David had been humbled throughout his life. He knew no man could love God without the help of God. The people respected David for this, and they listened to his counsel. Likewise, if we desire people to receive what we have to say, they need to feel our humility like the people felt David's. To help others, we absolutely must be humble. Pride repels God and people.

Psalm 51:16-17 seems a bit out of place at first glance. But Psalm 51:16 begins with "For," which means that there is a connection between the verses before it. In Psalm 51:13-15, David is proclaiming his desire to love God and love people through the power of his Lord. Now in Psalm 51:16-17, David says, "For you will not delight in sacrifice, or I would give it; you will not be pleased with a burnt offering. The sacrifices of God are a broken spirit; a broken and contrite heart, O God, you will not despise."

David's sacrifice to God is not burnt offerings. It's his promises of public praise and service found in Psalm 51:13-15. David is seeking to love God by loving those whom God loves. David knows what God's heart aches for. Therefore the gift David desires to give God is the lost people who God desires to transform, just like he did for David. God won't delight in animal sacrifice from David, but he will delight in the people David is seeking to love on God's behalf.

Likewise, Paul states, "For what is our hope, our joy, or the crown in which we will glory in the presence of our Lord Jesus when he comes? Is it not you?" (1 Thessalonians 2:19). Paul spent his life on earth preparing a gift to give to the God who saved him, and that gift was the people Paul helped to know Christ better.

God desires the same gift from us. David was a former adulterer and murder. Paul was a former persecutor of the church. God used these men to instruct transgressors and turn sinners back to him. You may feel God could never use you to help others. But just as he did with these two men, God desires to use us in helping others because the power and the results depend on him. You won't get the glory anyway, so don't worry about how unworthy you are. In their own merit, no one is worthy to serve God. Thankfully, Jesus makes us worthy and uses us because of his grace.

Helping others is not our way of getting God to love us again. Rather, because we know God loves us, now we have the desire to help others as he and others have helped us. Sexual sin involves using others, not loving them. Therefore, turning and repenting from sexual sin should include loving other humans. We are not repenting so we will be forgiven, but because God has forgiven us, now our heart's true desire is to repent and turn the other direction.

God doesn't need your good works as a sacrifice for your sins. He desires our good works as a sacrifice resulting from the grace he's given us. We will never love God and others without God's grace. He alone can humble our hearts. And when he does, we will then listen and do our Master's will.

Going Deeper

1. What's the danger of emphasizing good works without emphasizing God's grace (Ephesians 2:8-10)?

2. What's the danger of emphasizing God's grace without emphasizing good works (Ephesians 2:8-10)?

3. Do you find yourself trying to do what God desires because he loves you or so that he will love you? Do you think there is a difference?

4. If someone was to ask you to help them overcome their sexual sin, what would be your first thought? Often our first thought is evidence of what we are letting define us. Are you defined by your past sins or are you defined by your Savior? What's holding you back from helping others?

5. Read 2 Corinthians 1:8-12. How do Paul's past experiences with God give him confidence in the present? How can our past experiences of grace help us in the present?

6. What similarities do you see between Psalm 51 and Psalm 40?

7. How does humility help us teach and love others?

8. If God doesn't need our good works, why does he use us to produce good works for him?

9. Why do you think it is so important that we not only seek to find freedom from sexual sins ourselves, but that we also seek to help others do the same?

10. Even if you are actively struggling in certain areas of your sexuality while also seeking to repent, God has still shown you grace and love. If you have made progress and are no longer committing the sexual sins you once did, certainly you have good news to share with others. In either case, write out some of the blessings God has shown you that you can share with other people who may be struggling like you have in the past.

Chapter 10: Helping Heal Those You've Hurt

Psalm 51:18-19
Do good to Zion in your good pleasure; build up the walls of Jerusalem; [19] *then will you delight in right sacrifices, in burnt offerings and whole burnt offerings; then bulls will be offered on your altar.*

As much as we like to think that our sin only affects us, it simply does not. All sin, whether directly or indirectly, always affects more than just the person who sinned. Never was this demonstrated so clearly than through King David's sin with Bathsheba. Nathan prophesied to David:

> You have struck down Uriah the Hittite with the sword and have taken his wife to be your wife and have killed him with the sword of the Ammonites. [10] Now therefore the sword shall never depart from your house, because you have despised me and have taken the wife of Uriah the Hittite to be your wife.' [11] Thus says the LORD, 'Behold, I will raise up evil against you out of your own house. And I will take your wives before your eyes and give them to your neighbor, and he shall lie with your wives in the sight of this sun. [12] For you did it secretly, but I will do this thing before all Israel and before the sun.'" [13] David said to Nathan, "I have sinned against the LORD." And Nathan said to David, "The LORD also has put away your sin; you shall

not die. [14] Nevertheless, because by this deed you have utterly scorned the LORD, the child who is born to you shall die." [15] Then Nathan went to his house. (2 Samuel 12:9-15)

So much can be said about these verses above, but for our purposes in this Bible study on Psalm 51, all I will say is this: Even though bad things happened because of David's sins, this does not nullify the fact that God was still utterly faithful to David, just as he is to us when we sin and experience consequences. It may seem like God didn't grant David grace, but the fact that God didn't kill David because of his sin says otherwise. Even when God allows the consequences of our sins to affect us, he is still with us, desires good for us, and desires to use for good what was meant for evil.

Sometimes we can be confused when God does not spare us of the consequences of our sins. If God is forgiving and gracious, why does he allow our sins to hurt us and hurt others? Answers to questions like these need a book of their own. Perhaps the most concise way to answer this is with an analogy. Let's say for the last six months, you've been committing gluttony. Then you come to your senses, repent, ask for God's grace through Jesus Christ, and then God completely redeems and forgives you. The fat you gained, however, remains. Just because God forgives and shows grace does not mean he's going to magically take away the extra 50lbs you gained during your six months of living a gluttonous life.

God will indeed help you recover, but you are not going to wake up with a six-pack the morning after you repent. God will help you escape the consequences of your gluttony (the 50lbs) by teaching you self-control, healthy eating habits, and how to honor him with your body through exercise. This same principle can be applied to the consequences of all our other sins as well.

God redeems and completely wipes our debts clean, but sometimes, just like the extra pounds we put on through gluttony, the consequences remain. When it comes to sexual sins, so often the natural consequences of our rebellion affect other people.

When you commit adultery, you are deeply wounding your wife, your kids, and the family of the other person you have committed adultery with. When you have premarital sex, you are hurting your future spouse, your current boyfriend or girlfriend, and their future spouse. When you lust over porn, you are perpetuating the abuse of others, creating a world in your head that isn't real, and using sex as a weapon that will eventually wound those you love. When you masturbate, you are being self-centered and using sex to serve yourself rather than the person God has for you.

Even though God completely forgives and transforms us from all our past sexual sin once we repent and seek his grace, there's always a trail of people we've hurt. David knew this, and so he did what we all must seek to do. He tried to help heal those he hurt.

Don't Do Anything That Will Make the Damage Worse

Before we start talking about how to help heal those we've hurt through our sexual sin, we must first pray for the discernment necessary so we don't make the damage even worse. Each situation will need a different approach, so I encourage each of you to walk with God on this, consult the Scriptures, and appeal to common sense. With that said, here are a few pointers when seeking to heal those you've sexually sinned against.

If contacting a certain person will only tempt you and them to reengage in an unhealthy relationship you know God is telling you to stay clear of, then it's best to simply pray for that person's healing. Sometimes there is so much negative history between two people, the best way to help the healing process is to keep your distance. 1 Corinthians 6:18 states, "Flee from sexual immorality." Like Joseph who was tempted by Potiphar's wife, sometimes the best choice is to just run away (Genesis 39:8-12).

Be honest with yourself. If you know you need to apologize, then don't use this as a copout. If there's the remotest possibility seeking to apologize to this person will lead to more sins, like arguing or sexual temptation, then be smart and stay away. Some relationships were so combustible and heated, it's best to just keep your distance, pray for that person, and confess your sins to the Lord rather than poke the hornet's nest.

If your previous boyfriend or girlfriend is dating someone else, out of respect for the new relationship, you should not seek to directly apologize to that person for your sexual sin. Forgive them of any wrongs and pray that they will forgive you too. Due to the type of sin involved in your relationship with that person, the best way to help them is to stay away.

This advice is doubly important if this person is now married. Pray that Christ will redeem all parties involved so that everyone will be a new creation in Christ, being sanctified day by day. Pray that everyone will forgive each other and enjoy the forgiveness, newness, and purity that God gives. Once you do, move on and allow everyone else to do the same. When God redeems our dead past, the only thing left to do is to treat it for what it is – dead.

If you feel there is a relationship where sexual sin occurred and that person is not in a new relationship, sometimes the Holy Spirit will lead us to apologize directly to him or her. Pray about how to do this. Be thoughtful. Consider if a phone call, a letter, or an in-person meeting will be most beneficial.

Don't use this as an opportunity for manipulation to try and get someone back in your life. If God wants to use your repentance to reignite a relationship, he will do this. It's okay if that's the end result, but it's important for you to have a pure motivation which is centered on pleasing God and genuinely helping heal the people you've hurt.

If you are not married or engaged but you are in a dating relationship, have caution on how much you confide in your dating partner about your sexual struggles. When it comes to confessing sins such as porn use and masturbation, in most cases your girlfriend or boyfriend is not the person you should be talking with. This may be asking more than a dating relationship is meant to handle.

If you're drawing closer to marriage, you should confide in them that sexual sin and lust are a weakness for you so they know who they are marrying. Don't, however, ask them to be your counselor or accountability partner. If you feel the need to confide in them about your sexual sins of the past you committed with others, again, be cautions. If marriage is in the future, a conversation will need to be had, but do not get into details. Keep the conversation as general as possible without being dishonest about the sins of your past.

If you've sexually sinned against your spouse, you absolutely need to confess your sins directly to him or her. With that said, I personally don't believe your spouse should be your daily, weekly, or monthly accountability partner. Men and women's sexual struggles are often so different, it's hard for your spouse to understand. If you've committed adultery, you must confess but without going into graphic detail. Seek the help of a good, Christian counselor to help you and your spouse begin the healing process.

When it comes to porn, lust, and masturbation, my personal belief is that your spouse should know of your struggle. If you've never confessed these sins to him or her, you should. But I don't believe it is healthy to confess these types of sins in great detail and every single time you struggle.

For example: If you are a husband, your wife needs to know you struggle with lust. She doesn't need to know that when you were at the grocery store and you saw the cover of a magazine, you played out a fantasy in your head. She needs to know you struggle late at night with internet porn. She doesn't need to know what specific types of pictures and videos you have looked at.

You need to confess every sin you are aware of to God. Your spouse is not God. He or she can't handle the pressure of being your spouse, your pastor, your accountability partner, your best friend, and let alone your God. If you feel a conviction by the Holy Spirit to act otherwise and share more with your spouse, I am certainly not seeking to get in the way of that conviction. My warning is that you should be wise and prayerful about this. You need to repent to your spouse, confess to your spouse, and let your spouse know about your struggles. But giving lots of details and making this a daily conversation is not healthy.

Don't use my words as an excuse to ignore what you feel the Holy Spirit is leading you to do. Pray about what God is leading you to do and obey.

David Repented Publicly

Remember, David could have kept Psalm 51 tucked away in the pages of his personal journal. That's not what he did. He published this psalm for the world to read. Perhaps he figured since his sin was so public and affected so many people, his repentance should be as equally public. This is a good rule of thumb: The openness of your repentance should reflect the level of how public the sin was. If you've sinned in your mind, you probably don't need to tell too many people. If you are a leader of a church and everyone was affected by your sin, only apologizing to God in your mind is not the only step you should take.

Some of you may think if you told your spouse what you've done they would never forgive you. That may be true, but that's not your concern. Nothing binds a husband and wife together like forgiveness. Marriage is a reflection of Christ and his Bride, the Church. The Church's relationship with God is founded on the cross, love, and forgiveness; our marriages with our spouse should be no different if we desire to reflect Christ and his Bride.

We can't force people to forgive us. We can't guarantee someone will choose to allow God's healing to take place. We are only responsible for doing what we can. Like David, we should seek to help heal those we've hurt.

How to Help Others Forgive You

Psalm 51:18, "Do good to Zion in your good pleasure; build up the walls of Jerusalem . . . ."

King David's sin hurt others. In the end of his prayer of repentance, he remembers those he's wounded and harmed. One of the first ways David helped the people of Israel was by seeking his own personal healing and growth. As the leader of the nation, David's backsliding or forward progress always directly affected the people. Likewise, we all have other people we are responsible to lead, help, and love. The first way we must seek to love them is by taking care of ourselves and dealing with our own destructive issues, like our chronic sexual sin patterns.

Next, the help we seek to give those we've hurt must be rooted in God's love, not our own need for others to forgive us. David prayed in Psalm 51:18, "Do good to Zion in your good pleasure." Do you remember how Psalm 51:1 started? It reads, ". . . according to your steadfast love; according to your abundant mercy blot out my transgressions." David is seeking to love those he's hurt in the way that God has loved him. God loves, forgives, and blesses people because of his "good pleasure," "steadfast love," and "abundant mercy."

To help mend others, David is focusing on God. He does this because he knows we have no control over other people. As hard as we try not to, we all sin against those we love. Sometimes it is difficult for them to forgive us. Whether it's because we keep sinning against them the same way or because the sin we confessed was so hurtful, there are times in life when we will confess our sins to those we have hurt, but they will struggle to forgive us.

Thankfully the Bible talks a lot about forgiveness. Here are five truths found in Scripture that will help answer the questions, "How do I get someone to forgive me?"

1. Ask for Forgiveness. Don't Force It. Forgiveness Is Their Choice

Biblically speaking, it's actually impossible "to get someone to forgive you" or "make someone forgive you." True forgiveness, like love, is always a choice each individual must make within their own heart. Our relationship with God should be the blueprint for our relationship with others.

When we sin against God, we don't "get" or "make" Jesus forgive us. Jesus forgives us because he chooses to, because he desires it, and because it is in his character to offer grace when we don't deserve it.

When we try to force people to forgive us, it hardens their heart even more. The first thing we should do when we want forgiveness is ask the person we sinned against. The next thing we must do is allow them the freedom to do whatever they decide. Even if they don't forgive us when we ask, which is against God's will (Matthew 18:22), we must allow them the freedom to do what they want. We can't shove the Bible back in their face and expect them to jump at the opportunity to have affectionate and warm feelings towards us. Therefore, to get someone to forgive you, you must allow that person the time they need to obey God by their own free choice.

2. Truly Repent and Be Genuine

God has placed the burden of reconciliation on both the offender and the offended, so no one can do something to force the other party to forgive. But it sure helps the human heart move on from being offended when the offender is truly repenting and is genuinely sorry for their sins. Ephesians 4:25, 29 states:

> "Therefore, having put away falsehood, let each one of you speak the truth with his neighbor, for we are members one of another. . . . [29]Let no corrupting talk come out of your mouths, but only such as is good for building up, as fits the occasion, that it may give grace to those who hear."

These verses explain that what you say can positively and negatively affect other people. When we speak the truth in love, it benefits those who are willing to hear it. Only when we are repenting and genuinely seeking to "put away falsehood" will we be of any service in helping others love and obey God. If you are still living in your sin, you will be of no help to the person you want forgiveness from because they will know your repentance is not genuine.

3. Focus on Yourself and Receive the Rebuke

In Luke 17:3-4 Jesus instructs us to, "Pay attention to yourselves! If your brother sins, rebuke him, and if he repents, forgive him, and if he sins against you seven times in the day, and turns to you seven times, saying, 'I repent,' you must forgive him."

Again, to help others we must pay attention to ourselves. Additionally, we must be willing to receive a rebuke from those we've hurt. When we sin against someone, it is their biblical right to loving rebuke us. This does not mean they have the freedom to blast us, to be rude to us, or to sinfully judge us (which would be judging our hearts rather than our actions). But they are to righteously judge our external sins (1 Corinthians 5:12-13) and rebuke us when we error against him or her (Luke 17:3).

We must allow them their biblical right to correct us because we then have the biblical right to be forgiven. In Luke 17:3-4 Jesus tells the person who is wronged to rebuke *and* to forgive. If you as the offender want the forgiveness, you must also be willing to receive the loving rebuke.

4. Allow Them to Be Angry

There is an anger that is not sin. Ephesians 4:26 explains, "Be angry and do not sin; do not let the sun go down on your anger, and give no opportunity to the devil." God gets angry over sin (Colossians 3:6). There is a time and place for Christians to do the same. When we hurt, violate, misuse, and sin against someone, it is a right response on their part to have a righteous anger over this.

However, God does not remain angry if the sinner repents and relies on the gospel of Jesus Christ. God is always looking for ways to be reconciled to his enemies. Christians must imitate God. Ephesians 4:26 explains that there is a righteous anger, but it also explains that Christians must not linger and hold on to any anger for an extended period of time. If we want people to forgive us, we must allow them the time to be righteously angry over our sins against them so that they can then move on, forgive us, and "not let the sun go down" on their anger against us.

5. Pray for Them

Lastly and most importantly, if we want someone to forgive us, we must pray for them. Romans 8:26-27 states:

> "Likewise the Spirit helps us in our weakness. For we do not know what to pray for as we ought, but the Spirit himself intercedes for us with groanings too deep for words. And he who searches hearts knows what is the mind of the Spirit, because the Spirit intercedes for the saints according to the will of God."

When someone's heart is hard towards us, we are completely powerless to change this. People have no power over other people's hearts. Changing the human heart belongs solely to the Holy Spirit. He alone has the power to change, soften, and heal our hearts.

When someone won't forgive you, it is the most powerless feeling in the world. The only action to take when someone won't forgive you is to pray for them. You may not even know what to pray, "but the Spirit himself intercedes for us with groanings too deep for words."

David prayed in Psalm 51:18, "Do good to Zion in your good pleasure; build up the walls of Jerusalem." In other words, David is praying for only what God can produce. He knows the future of Zion is in the hands of God, just as we must humbly admit that we are powerless to truly heal those we've hurt. We have a part to play in this healing process, but it really is in the hands of God.

Dealing With Those Who Want To Harm You

We've talked about how to deal with the people we've hurt, but what about the people who want to hurt us?

Sexual sin, especially when it included another person you had a significant relationship with, is a breeding ground for hatred. Relationships that started with sexual sin and were sustained by sexual sin always end in anger, frustration, and hatred.

As we've discussed previously, humans often sexualize their feelings. One feeling that is often at the root of sinful sexual expression is anger towards others. To overcome sexual temptation and take a giant leap forward on your journey to freedom, one of the greatest steps you can take is to forgive those who have hurt you and deal with any lingering anger you have towards those who hate you.

Whenever David failed, certain people were happy about this. One of the consequences to David's sin with Bathsheba was the rebellion of David's son Absalom. Absalom was successful for a short period of time in taking over David's kingdom. When David and those loyal to him were retreating from Absalom, a man named Shimei was overjoyed by David's trouble. Shimei was from the family of Saul (an adversary to David), and as David retreated, Shimei ridiculed, cursed, and threw rocks at him and his people (2 Samuel 16:5-6).

If David's shame over his sin with Bathsheba was not enough, now other people were rubbing his face in it. Saul, Absalom, and now Shimei all deserved David's wrath. David was a man of war. If he wanted to destroy these men, he and his mighty warriors could have bathed themselves in their blood. But David took a different route.

David could have easily killed Saul twice. Instead he said to Saul, "May the LORD judge between you and me. And may the LORD avenge the wrongs you have done to me, but my hand will not touch you. As the old saying goes, 'From evildoers come evil deeds,' so my hand will not touch you" (1 Samuel 24:12-13, NIV).

David's men wanted to kill Shimei, but David said, "Leave him alone, and let him curse . . . It may be that the LORD will look on the wrong done to me, and that the LORD will repay me with good for his cursing today" (2 Samuel 16:11-12). When the time came for David to take back his kingdom, he said to his men, "Deal gently for my sake with the young man Absalom" (2 Samuel 18:5).

In life, people often deserve our hatred, our anger, and our unforgiveness. And yet when we give people the evil they deserve, the person we are hurting the most is ourselves. Proverbs 11:17 states, "A man who is kind benefits himself, but a cruel man hurts himself."

God will punish those who seek our harm, or he will take their punishment and put it on Christ if they put their faith in the gospel. No one is getting away with anything. The only thing we accomplish when we take matters into our own hands is our own harm. The proper response to those who seek to do us harm is David's, "And may the LORD avenge the wrongs you have done to me, but my hand will not touch you. As the old saying goes, 'From evildoers come evil deeds,' so my hand will not touch you" (1 Samuel 24:12-13, NIV).

If David would have sinned against those who sinned against him, he knew the only thing he would have proved was that he was evil like them. But by sparing those who deserved punishment, David benefited himself. Like Christ, who humbled himself on the cross for our sake and who was then honored with the name that is above every name (Philippians 2:5-11), so we too are benefited when we lay ourselves down and treat people better than they deserve (Matthew 5:43-48).

God Is Always The Greatest Gift

Psalm 51:19, " . . . then will you delight in right sacrifices, in burnt offerings and whole burnt offerings; then bulls will be offered on your altar."

The last way David seeks to help others is through praying and hoping that they will experience the very best blessing: A flourishing relationship with God.

When David prays that God would "delight in [the people's] right sacrifices," he is expressing his desire for the people's relationship with God to be redeemed like his was. David wanted the people to experience his greatest joy, his greatest passion – a right relationship with God.

When David mentions "whole burnt offerings," he's expressing his hope that the people will love God lavishly. Some offerings were partially burned before the Lord while the rest of the sacrifice was to be given to the priests and the people. However, a burnt offering was to be totally consumed by the fire as a complete offering to God (except for the hide). Additionally, the "bulls" were costlier than a normal sacrifice like a ram or lamb.

David desired Israel to offer lavish sacrifices and whole burnt offerings because he wanted the people to live the best life possible, a life given to God in "whole." David desired the best for the people; therefore David desired them to be completely committed to the Lord with all their heart.

The greatest gift God ever gives us is the gift of himself. An intimate relationship with God our Savior is like nothing else. Therefore, as we seek to help and heal those we've hurt through our sexual sin, may our greatest desire be that they personally experience God like never before.

Going Deeper

1. What are your immediate reactions to this chapter? What parts do you agree and disagree with? Why?

2. How has your sexual sin hurt other people, directly and indirectly?

3. Why do you think God doesn't always save us from consequences even though he always forgives us?

4. Why should every Christian seek to forgive those who have sinned against them while also seeking the forgiveness of those they have sinned against?

5. Why is it so hard to love our enemies? What's one lesson you have learned from David on how to treat your enemy?

6. Why is prayer so essential when it comes to forgiveness and inner healing?

7. Read Psalm 51:16 and Psalm 51:19. Why does God not delight in burnt offerings in Psalm 51:16 but does delight in them in Psalm 51:19? What's the difference between how these sacrifices are offered?

8. Do you believe a husband and wife should be each other's daily accountability partner? If one spouse struggles with porn or masturbation, how often do you think he or she should communicate about this with the other spouse?

9. List everyone you believe your sexual sin has hurt. Pray about if you should contact any of these people to apologize to or if you should simply pray for their healing.

10. Write out a prayer of protection and healing for your marriage (or future marriage). Ask God to protect your marriage from sexual sin, heal your marriage from the sexual sin, and grow your marriage so both you and your spouse will be able to love each other well and enjoy God together. (If you feel God has led you to live a celibate life, pray about this instead.)

Conclusion: Never Give UP

David was remembered for many great things, but his sin with Bathsheba was never erased from the history books. 1 Kings 15:4-5 states, "Nevertheless, for David's sake the LORD his God gave him a lamp in Jerusalem, setting up his son after him, and establishing Jerusalem, because David did what was right in the eyes of the LORD and did not turn aside from anything that he commanded him all the days of his life, except in the matter of Uriah the Hittite." God no longer held it against him, but through David's life this sin was always attached to his story.

There are times in life when we just want to run away from the mistakes we've made. It would have been so easy for King David to cast Bathsheba from his presence, only looking at her as a reminder of his own failures. But that's not what David did. Although their relationship started in sin, David knew that repentance means running from your sin and not from your responsibilities to do what's right.

As bad as David's rebellion was, the way he repented is what reminds us of David's true character. 2 Samuel 11-12 recounts what happened between David and Bethsheba. 2 Samuel 13, however, shares the details of a similar story but with a very different ending. David had a son, Amnon, who had an obsession with Tamar. To make a long story short, Amnon sexually violated her. After he did so, 2 Samuel 13:15-17 explains:

"Then Amnon hated her with very great hatred, so that the hatred with which he hated her was greater than the love with which he had loved her. And Amnon said to her, "Get up! Go!" [16] But she said to him, "No, my brother, for this wrong in sending me away is greater than the other that you did to me." But he would not listen to her. [17] He called the young man who served him and said, "Put this woman out of my presence and bolt the door after her.""

Some believe David raped Bathsheba as Amnon did to Tamar. I personally do not believe this since in 2 Samuel 13, where rape did occur, Scripture makes it clear. If David raped Bathsheba, it seems Scripture would have made that clear too. Nonetheless, the point to truly see here is how different David and Amnon responded once they were convicted over their sexual sin. Amnon did not want to truly repent. He just wanted to run away from his shame and never be reminded of his failures again.

David didn't treat Bathsheba this way (1 Kings 1:28-31). Surely when he looked at her he was sometimes reminded of his past failures, but David knew true repentance is doing the next right action. After we sin sexually, many of us just want to run away and act like it never happened. Perhaps your sinful sexual past led to an abortion, a divorce, an out of wedlock birth, a broken relationship, or some shameful memory. If we hope to be free from sexual temptation in the future, we have to do the next right action. We can't just abandon the issues we've created through our rebellion.

Like David, if we hope to be men and women after God's own heart, we need to be known not for our perfections but for how we repented after our imperfections were exposed.

You Will Stumble, But You Don't Have to Fall

I'd love to tell you that if you do everything I talked about in this book, I can guarantee you will never fall to sexual temptation ever again. I would love to gift wrap a 10-step plan to absolute sexual purity and put a little bow on it. I simply can't do that.

I want to encourage you by giving you a look into the future: You will stumble again to sexual temptation at some point in your life. Wait . . . what? How is that supposed to help you? I am certainly not insinuating that it's okay if you fall to sexual temptation. I'm just letting you know that you will sin again in some form or other. As you are being sanctified in Christ you will sin less and less, but all of us will still struggle to some degree. Here's the encouraging part: If you always repent, God will always redeem and continue to grow you.

The key to gaining more and more freedom (sanctification) in the battle against sexual temptation is to never give up. You are going to fail, but with the endless grace of Jesus Christ, you don't ever have to be a failure. Psalm 37:23-24 states, "The LORD makes firm the steps of the one who delights in him; though he may stumble, he will not fall, for the LORD upholds him with his hand." John comforts his readers when he states:

"If we say we have no sin, we deceive ourselves, and the truth is not in us. If we confess our sins, he is faithful and just to forgive us our sins and to cleanse us from all unrighteousness. If we say we have not sinned, we make him a liar, and his word is not in us.

My little children, I am writing these things to you so that you may not sin. But if anyone does sin, we have an advocate with the Father, Jesus Christ the righteous. He is the propitiation for our sins, and not for ours only but also for the sins of the whole world." (1 John 1:8-10, 1 John 2:1-2)

Don't Give Up

What is the most important advice you can tell a Christian who struggles with sexual temptation? Well if they are a true Christian, we can assume they already know the fundamentals of the faith regarding Christ and the gospel (see chapters 4-6). Therefore, the most important counsel to know is that you must never give up.

It sounds so simple, but once we understand and accept the truth about Jesus Christ, Satan's only ploy left is to get us to turn back around and give up. We live in a season where the war is won but the battles rage on.

Therefore, if we simply keep believing, repenting of sin, and straining towards Christ's will for us, our lives cannot end in defeat. However, if we let go of our faith, turn our back on God, or simply give up pursuing the gifts Jesus has already won for us, only then can we be defeated as this would prove we were never truly redeemed in the first place (1 John 2:19).

The only unforgivable sin is the sin that we no longer repent from. I'm not saying we are doomed to hell if we sin and then forget that we sinned, thus never specifically confessing to God one particular sin in our past. No, Jesus died once for all of our sins (Hebrews 9:28, 1 Peter 3:18).

However, repentance means to turn the other direction, to no longer go on sinning as we once did. Therefore, the only sin that will not be forgiven is the sin we never turn from, the sin we ultimately choose over God. If you stop fighting a certain sexual sin and it completely takes your desire away to pursue God – that is what cannot be forgiven. You cannot be reeled in by a lifeline you just severed. This is why it is so essential that no matter how many times you run, you always repent. You must never give up.

Again, when someone runs but doesn't come back to God, this does not mean they lost their salvation. It means, rather, that they never had a true salvation to begin with (1 John 2:19). Colossians 1:21-23 explains:

> "Once you were alienated from God and were enemies in your minds because of your evil behavior. But now he has reconciled you by Christ's physical body through death to present you holy in his sight, without blemish and free from accusation— if you continue in your faith, established and firm, and do not move from the hope held out in the gospel."

Let us "not move from the hope held out in the gospel." The victory is ours, we just have to finish the race. So no matter how many times you fail, no matter how many times you are betrayed by others, no matter how many times you turn from God, no matter how many times life does not work out the way you had hoped, what is of the utmost importance is that you do not give up and you always turn back to God, seeking him above everything else.

Don't ever let sexual sin keep you down. You will stumble, but by the grace of God you don't ever have to completely fall. You can always get back up, be redeemed, and grow into the man or woman God has designed you to be.

God's Great Warriors Are Great at Repentance

I think we are all looking for the "zap" effect. We want God to zap us and bang, the anger's gone, the lust is gone, you're a perfect dad, you're a perfect husband, you're the ideal Christian man.

We sometimes hear about someone's out of body worship experience, how in one momentous moment they were transformed and now this person lives on top of the mountain. Naturally we want that too. The regular pattern in Scripture, however, is that when we put our faith in Jesus, he gives us his Holy Spirit, we become a new creation, we are justified, but then the rest of our lives are spent learning how to love God more and more. Our life changes day by day through our ever deepening relationship with our Father.

David was anointed as king as a young teenager, but after his anointing he was sent back out into the field to walk through sheep dung and to fight off wild animals. Then he fought Goliath, then he served in King Saul's army, then he became a general, then he became king of Judah, and then he became king over all of Israel. Life truly is a journey.

Even after David's sin with Bathsheba, he continued to make mistakes. One such mistake was when he took a census, putting his trust in numbers rather than in God. 2 Samuel 24:10 states, "But David's heart struck him after he had numbered the people. And David said to the LORD, 'I have sinned greatly in what I have done. But now, O LORD, please take away the iniquity of your servant, for I have done very foolishly.'"

Just as there were still natural consequences for David's rebellion with Bathsheba, there were consequences following his census. Despite all that, God still redeemed David from his sin once he repented. The mark of God's greatest warriors is not sinlessness but rather their sincere repentance after they sin. You can be a great warrior for God, but your greatness will have less to with your perfections and much more to do with how you deal with your imperfections.

David's future was never defined by his past. David knew his greatness was always directly tied to God's mercy and love. Because he placed all his hope in God his Savior, he was not ruined by his own rebellion.

David's love for God was seen in his obedience, but perhaps it was seen even more in how he dealt with his own disobedience. No matter how far David ran, he always came sprinting back to God harder and faster. His devotion to God was tested when he faced temptation, but it was tested even more after he failed the test of temptation. David's greatness can be seen best in how he depended on God. David loved God much because he had been forgiven much.

Our failures are not at the center of the story. God our Savior is at the center of the story. God's grace and glory are always at center stage. God's ultimate plan for your life does not depend on your perfections but on his sovereignty and power. Our God is able to redeem the worst of situations . . . as long as we don't give up.

David always repented after he sinned. If we hope to be redeemed like David, we must do the same. God loves you and desires good for you. Always seek after him.

Redeemed Like David Leader's Guide

Introduction

Redeemed Like David has been written for individuals, accountability partners, and small group Bible studies. This leader's guide will help anyone or any group go even deeper.

I've tried to write this leader's guide in a casual way. I hope you feel that I am right there with you, helping you understand the concepts and truths of Psalm 51 which we have specifically applied to fighting sexual temptation.

To help support you and connect with you, I encourage you to check out our additional resources found at ApplyGodsWord.com. This is our central hub for all of our content and resources. If you want to connect with me (Mark Ballenger) personally, ask questions, and get a ton of free resources that are meant to help you love God and people better, definitely check out what we are doing at AGW Ministries.

Throughout my answers to the questions we will be discussing, I have also given you practical advice on how to lead a small group/accountability partnership. Here are a few more general pointers that will help:

- Be wise in how you approach these topics depending on what type of relationship you have with the other people you are studying with. If you are studying this with your best friend, jump right in and be as open as possible. If you are studying this as a church small group Bible study with people who don't know each other that well, go slow. Perhaps use the first night to get to know one another socially.

- Obviously, when it comes to sexual sin and temptation, this can be a sensitive subject. Don't embarrass people by asking them to make known all their struggles, especially if the group is new. If people signed up for a small group Bible study, then let the accountability happen as an overflow of this group. Let people confide in one another at their own pace. If you and your accountability partner said you would be as honest as possible, go for it. If you asked people to sign up for a class and not a support group, then keep it content centered and let people make their own choice on how much they want to reveal about their struggles. Set the expectations and don't blow through them.

- When you ask a question, don't feel the need to immediately answer it if no one else does. Often times it will take a minute of silence before a group member feels he or she should share. If the group is especially quiet, call on someone you know who won't be offended. If one person always answers and talks too much, think of creative ways to get others involved. Perhaps assign one question per week to each person in the small group, go around the circle, or ask one person a week to come up with a bonus question. Keep people engaged.

- This book was designed to be applicable for both men and women who struggle with sexual temptation, lust, porn, masturbation, and other similar sins. However, I believe it is best to study this topic not in a coed environment. I believe when it comes to talking about sexual temptations, mixing genders has a potential for serious complications and a lack of honesty/integrity.

- As the leader, be prepared, but don't kill yourself. Again, live up to the expectations you set at the beginning. If you are teaching this as a class, you'll need to spend extra time in preparation. If you are facilitating a small group Bible study, come up with some bonus questions in case your group flies through the questions provided. If you are leading a support group, think about how you will navigate difficult personalities. I recommend you don't meet for more than two hours at a time. I've found that one hour and thirty minutes is usually plenty of time if the group stays focused and on task.

- Don't feel like you have to get through every question. Feel free to pick and choose which ones you feel will benefit you and your group/accountability partnership the most. Supplement the material with your own questions and content when you feel it will help. Each group is different. You know your group better than me. This study guide and questions are just a starting point. Try to find the balance of staying on topic but allowing the Holy Spirit to lead the group each week where he wants. If the group naturally starts engaging about an issue not mentioned for that week, let it roll until it becomes unfruitful and too disorganized. In general, however, it's usually most fruitful to try and keep the group on topic.

- Make the environment as friendly and relaxing as possible. I know you love your dog, but some people in your group probably don't. Put away pets during the study time. Try to have some refreshments and snacks. Perhaps create a weekly signup sheet for people to help provide food and drinks. Allow for social time before and after the group. Don't make every minute of your time together super heavy and emotionally exhausting.

- There's a lot more that could be said, but overall, just use common sense. Be a great host, go the extra mile to love people, and be prepared. Your small group, class, Bible study, or accountability partner will appreciate you and return the love.

Going Deeper Chapter 1

1. What's typically your first reaction after you commit a sexual sin?

It's a good sign when you feel guilty and convicted after you commit a sexual sin. God blesses us with a holy conviction over our rebellion when the Holy Spirit is in us.

In my past sexual sins, I've typically been eager to make it right. Often I've made rash promises that I will never sin like that again. I've tried to beat myself up to prove to myself and God that I truly am sorry. As I've matured, I've realized that often times my attempt to beat myself up was often rooted in my desire to pay for my own sins. If I felt horrible enough, I reasoned, then God would forgive me and put me back in his good graces.

2. What should be your first reaction after you commit a sexual sin?

King David doesn't make promises to God. He relies on the promises of God. He doesn't try to cut a deal to pay for his sins. Instead he turns to God in prayer.

I believe our first reaction and movement towards repentance should start with prayer. If we repent by chucking our computer against the wall, calling our accountability partner, or make a promise that we will never sin like that again, often times we are seeking to rely on our actions for our redemption. These things are not wrong, but only God's grace will remove our guilt.

David's prayer of repentance starts with depending on the mercy and love of God (Psalm 51:1-2). When we truly desire to repent and be changed, we must turn to God personally, confess our sins, pray for the help needed to turn from evil, and then come up with a plan with the Lord on what actions steps we are going to take to overcome sexual sin.

1 John 1:9 gives us great directions on what to do after we sin, "If we confess our sins, he is faithful and just to forgive us our sins and to cleanse us from all unrighteousness."

3. What sin cycles have you been trapped in? Do you sin, feel shame, stay away from God, and then sin more because you are staying away from God? Or do you have a different sin pattern? How can you break your specific sin cycle?

Throughout my high school years, I was trapped in this very cycle. I was living in rebellion towards God. But I was a Christian, so I was miserable in my rebellion. I once heard from a preacher that unbelievers can live in rebellion towards God and have seasons of happiness and feel no guilt. When a Christian backslides, however, they are truly miserable. Often times our misery tempts us to seek comfort in wrong places, which only offers temporary relief and produces more depression.

I thought that to break out of this sin cycle, I had to stop sinning so I could be right with God again. While there certainly is some truth to this, a sin cycle will never stop based on stopping sin. You have to stop the cycle by going to God. You won't stop your sin and then get close to God. The closer you get to God through grace on a consistent base, the more your sin will stop.

Don't wait until you are perfect before you begin to pursue God. That time will never come. God is calling you right now. Go to him no matter what condition you are in. A relationship with him based on grace, repentance, and the gospel will truly set your free.

4. How do our past sexual failures affect our ability to fight sexual temptation in the future? Do you believe forgiveness of our past will lead to freedom in the future?

Our futures don't need to be defined by our pasts if we seek the grace of Jesus Christ. But our pasts are a good indicator of what we might struggle with in the future. By looking at our past mistakes, we can have an honest assessment of what we need to guard against in the future.

Additionally, if we have not dealt with our past sexual sins, it's like we have unhealed wounds on our heart. Until these wounds are healed, we will always be more susceptible in these certain areas. For example, Ephesians 4:26-27 says, "Do not let the sun go down while you are still angry, [27] and do not give the devil a foothold." While this passage of the Bible is dealing with anger, the same pattern can occur with sins like lust, masturbation, porn, and sexual promiscuity. When we don't deal with our issues, they turn into sins. When we don't deal with our sins, they turn into footholds for the devil to work in our life.

We need to renounce sin, repent, and always return to God as soon as possible so we do not allow the devil to get a foothold. Thus, I do believe forgiveness of our past will help lead us to freedom in our future.

5. Do you feel it is important to immediately repent after you sin rather than letting time go by? Why or why not?

Yes, I do believe it is far better to confess and repent as soon as you are able. Refer to the answer in question 4 for more details.

The longer we deny the conviction of the Holy Spirit, the harder our hearts become. You only have two paths in the Christian life: forward and backwards. The faster you repent the better.

C.S. Lewis said, "We all want progress, but if you're on the wrong road, progress means doing an about-turn and walking back to the right road; in that case, the man who turns back soonest is the most progressive."

6. Why is it essential to know that God's love and mercy are based in God's character and not our character?

This is so crucial because our character so often fails us while God's character never fails us. If God loved us because of us, we would be unlovable. In an effort to show the great love of God, the modern preacher often expresses the value of man by how much God sacrificed to save him. The logic goes like this, "God loved you so much, he died for you. You are so special to God, he will never stop loving you." While these statements are true, it is important to note that our value is not the cause of God's love but the result. God gives us value because he loves us. God made us in him image because he loves us. God didn't have to make us at all, thus it is illogical to state that our self-derived value causes God to do anything.

At first glance this can be deflating. But none of these facts contradict the truth that God really does love us immensely. We really do have immense value and we really are made in the image of God. The fact that God loves us because of his own character should be a great joy because it means we can never lose the love of God. We can never become unlovable because God will never cease to be love himself (1 John 4:8,16). Because God is love, he loves us. This will never change.

(For more on this idea, see: Daniel 9:18, Ezekiel 36:23-32, Romans 5:6-8)

7. If someone asked you, "What does the love of God look like?" how would you answer?

1 John 4:9, "In this the love of God was made manifest among us, that God sent his only Son into the world, so that we might live through him."

God is love (1 John 4:8) and Jesus is the exact image of God, "He is the image of the invisible God, the firstborn of all creation" (Colossians 1:15).

Love is not just words. Love is expressed in action through the Word, capital "W" (John 1:1), which is Jesus. John 1:14 states, "And the Word became flesh and dwelt among us, and we have seen his glory, glory as of the only Son from the Father, full of grace and truth."

8. What person in your life have you felt the most loved by? Why has his or her love impacted you more than others?

Most often those who have impacted us the most with their love are those who have loved us without conditions. When someone supports, encourages, and expresses their love for us only when we are doing exactly what they want, it's hard for us to feel truly loved by them. Of course if we are walking in sin, being disobedient, or doing something that is unhealthy, those who love us should show their displeasure with our choices. But there is a difference between being disappointed and not loving someone.

Those who we have felt the most love from are often the ones who have loved us as a reflection of how God loves us.

For me personally, my dad has always been one of the most loving people in my life. When I was younger and living in rebellion, I never felt he loved me less. When I decided to be a missionary, a teacher, and then a pastor, he always loved me unconditionally regardless if I was doing the things he would want me to do. He never condoned my sin, but he always showed his love for me no matter what.

My wife is another great example. She has loved me the most in life and she has never removed her love when I mess up.

9. When you struggle to receive God's forgiveness, is it because you think your sin is too big or because you think

God is too small or a combination of both? How can you combat these false beliefs? (See Romans 8:31-39)

Without a right perceptive on the greatness of God compared to our sin, we will often times struggle to receive forgiveness. Pride can manifest in many ways, but two of the most common are mentioned in this question. It is prideful to think that your sin is somehow greater than God's grace. We may be thinking we are expressing humility when we say things like, "God could never forgive someone like me." But in reality these are prideful statements because you are saying your sin is just too much for God. Why is your sin so special? Your sinful past is not greater than God's grace just as no human sin is ever greater than God's grace. God is bigger than your sin and your sin is smaller than God. True humility submits to this fact and does not seek to exalt oneself by thinking your sin is more special and greater than other people's sin.

Romans 8:37-39, "No, in all these things we are more than conquerors through him who loved us. [38] For I am sure that neither death nor life, nor angels nor rulers, nor things present nor things to come, nor powers, [39] nor height nor depth, nor anything else in all creation, will be able to separate us from the love of God in Christ Jesus our Lord."

10. Psalm 51:2 (ESV) states, "Wash me thoroughly from my iniquity." Psalm 51:2 (NIV) states, "Wash away all my iniquity." It says God can wash us "thoroughly" and he can wash away "all" our sins. Is there any specific sexual sin in your past or reoccurring lustful sin in your present that you feel God cannot forgive? If so, apply the truths we've been

studying in this passage. Confess it to God and believe his love, mercy, and grace are greater than all your failures.

Depending on the level of the relationships are already formed within your small group Bible study/accountability partnership, this question may or may not be worth answering together. If this is the first or second session you are meeting together, don't force people to confess these sins to one another. If your group has been meeting and you have the emotional equity with one another, then go for it.

Either way, encourage your group members to each write down what that specific sin might be for them. Often times people struggle in one or two very specific ways. Some people struggle with premarital sex while others would never dare to commit that sin. Those who don't struggle with premarital sex, however, could be addicted to porn or masturbation while those who struggle with premarital sex have never looked at porn at all.

Each sin carries with it a special shame. The longer it goes on, the harder it is to have hope that they will ever break free. But God wants us to never give up. His grace truly is great enough. If we struggle and yet truly repent each time, God absolutely wipes our slate clean. His mercy and grace can never run out.

God will set us free, but we can't give up when we fail.

Going Deeper Chapter 2

1. Are you convicted about your sexual sin? Why or why not?

Guilt, feeling sorry, and feeling badly about your sin are not the same thing as being convicted by the Holy Spirit. When the power of the Holy Spirit convicts you of your sin, it is impossible for you not to act. The Holy Spirit puts such a strong sense of how you have offended God, you are overwhelmed to the point where you naturally call out to God for relief and help. Conviction is something you feel deep inside of you, but then it bursts forth into action. When it comes to sin, including sexual sin, no one can produce this deep conviction except the Holy Spirit. You can feel guilty, badly, and he even sorry about your sin. But the Holy Spirit's conviction causes an urgent movement to do whatever you can to escape the clutches of sin you now know are truly killing you and those you love.

If you feel this way, what's changed? How do you and your group members explain why sometimes there is a stronger conviction in your heart than other times? If you or any of your group members don't feel the Holy Spirit's conviction, explore why. Have you hardened your heart from years of rebellion? Are you afraid of the Holy Spirit? Have you avoided the Holy Spirit because your theology hasn't allowed you to seek his help/filling? Do what you need to do to figure out why you don't have a strong conviction from the Holy Spirit over your sexual sin because your life depends on it.

2. How does the word of God help bring a healthy conviction from the Holy Spirit?

It had been a really long and annoying day. I was ready to order a sinful amount of food as I sat in the drive through of McDonalds, but after a long pause of silence, someone finally said through the speaker box, "Hold on just one minute." The wait turned out to be longer than just one minute . . . a fact that was adding to the annoyance I was trying to solve through fat calories.

As I sat there, I was forced to take a closer look at the menu board. If you look very closely, next to each of the items there is a super small font size of the calories: caramel frappe (520 calories, 28% daily fat), Big Mac (540 calories, 43% daily fat), small fry (230 calories, 17% daily fat), 4 piece nuggets (190 calories, 18% daily fat) . . . "Oh my" I thought to myself.

"Go ahead with your order . . . ."
"Aaaa, I'll just get a banana strawberry smoothie (210 calories, 1% fat daily fat) . . . ."

Being forced to take a closer look at that menu made me reconsider what I was about to do. In the same way, when we take a closer look at the consequences of our choices written in God's word, we almost always make a better decision (James 1:25).

The word of God tells us the truth about sin. It doesn't hide the deadly affects of evil in the tiniest font possible. When we spend time daily in God's word, truly taking the time to consider the punishments and rewards God offers when we accept grace and obey rather than rejecting grace and disobeying God, the right choice becomes much easier to make.

"But whoever looks intently into the perfect law that gives freedom, and continues in it—not forgetting what they have

heard, but doing it—they will be blessed in what they do"
(James 1:25)

3. How does the Church and other Christians help bring conviction?

Galatians 6:1-2, "Brothers and sisters, if someone is caught in a sin, you who live by the Spirit should restore that person gently. But watch yourselves, or you also may be tempted.
² Carry each other's burdens, and in this way you will fulfill the law of Christ."

Proverbs 11:30, "The fruit of the righteous is a tree of life, and whoever captures souls is wise."

1 Corinthians 5:12-13, "For what have I to do with judging outsiders? Is it not those inside the church whom you are to judge? ¹³ God judges those outside. "Purge the evil person from among you."

In each of the Bible verses above, we are given a slightly different approach on how Christians (the Church) are to help one another with overcoming sin. Some people may need a loving embrace. Others may need a strong reality check so they can see they are walking in sin and are going to hurt themselves deeply. And others may be so rebellious towards correction they will need to be cast out of a relationship with the Church so that they have a better chance of coming to their senses and repenting.

The Church helps individual Christians have conviction in a variety of ways. Preaching is also a huge way the Church helps us have conviction over sexual sin.

4. Do you see the benefits of having what has commonly been called an "accountability partner"? Do you see any potential problems that can happen within this relationship? Lastly, if you've had an accountability partner before, what were some good and bad lessons you learned about this type of relationship through your past experiences?

I do see the value of an accountability partner. Oftentimes we are blinded to certain areas of our life. Someone we trust who has an outside perspective can be very valuable. Additionally, being around people with similar goals helps us grow towards the goals we have. Proverbs 13:20, "Whoever walks with the wise becomes wise, but the companion of fools will suffer harm." Christians should correct other Christians when one of them is getting of God's path.

With that said, often time the term "accountability partner" gives off a unbiblical impression (in my opinion). Ultimately we are accountable to God. A relationship built on checking if the other person sinned is not a biblical friendship. Brothers and sisters in Christ should seek the Lord together (2 Timothy 2:22); often times this means they will need to correct each other when someone sins. But this is not the primary point of our relationships with other Christians. An accountability partner, however, has the potential to create such a relationship.

With those you are studying with, share about your experiences with other accountability partners. I personally have had both good and bad experiences. The relationships that have been most beneficial, however, have been those friendships where accountability and loving correction were simply a natural overflow of being good friends who were seeking the Lord together. Long term relationships won't last if they are built around the avoidance of sexual sin.

5. How can you find other people in your life who can help you pursue Christ and fight sexual temptation?

One of the best ways to attract godly friends is to seek to be godly yourself. We typically attract the type of people who are like us. We may want Christian friends who are seeking the Lord, but if we are the type of person who does not seek the Lord, those who are doing this will not naturally want to be our friends. There may be people who see you as a ministry, as someone who needs help. But that's not a friendship. A friendship is built on giving and taking, not just taking.

Also, it helps to place yourself in good environments. The odds of finding an accountability partner or a fellow Christian soldier somewhere out in the secular world is not likely. It's possible, but you have much better odds of building Christian friendships if you decide to spend your time where other Christians are (church, service opportunities, seminars, ministries, small group Bible studies, est.)

6. Have you ever ignored the Holy Spirit's conviction? What happened?

Throughout high school I was in a rebellious place towards God. During that time I had a guilt over my sin, but I struggled with acting on my desire to repent. I would often say I was sorry to God, but I did not make the necessary changes for my life and behavior to actually be different. During this season, my heart grew hard and calloused the more I ignored the Holy Spirit. The more you choose to reject his counsel, the less you will hear his counsel.

Thankfully the Lord did get a hold of me. It wasn't until I took a year off in between high school and college that I began to truly change. God sent me to Africa as a missionary during that time, thus giving me the opportunity to escape the old patters, friends, and sinful habits that were ruining my life.

7. If you don't believe something is wrong, you won't have conviction over it. Is there a sin in your life you don't think is really that bad? What does the Bible say about this?

Humans love to make excuses for sin. We love to justify our wrong behavior. When we know something is wrong, we often think there are excuses that make it not as wrong. If we can make excuses or convince ourselves a certain sin is not that bad, we will lose our conviction to fight this sin. Rather than make weird excuses in our head, we simply need to go read our Bibles and figure out what God has already said on the matter. When God declares something a sin, then we don't have to wonder. We just need to fight it.

The prime example of this that I see the most has to do with the sin of masturbation. There are countless excuses that people make for why it is okay to masturbate. Some say that masturbation is not talked about within the Bible. If you don't believe masturbation is truly wrong, you will have no desire to stop doing it. To stop masturbating, you first need to truly sit down and decide what you believe: Is it a sin or not? Only when you see it as sinful will you take the next steps in stopping this behavior.

(For a deeper discussion on why the Bible does declare masturbation a sin, read the article, "Does the Bible Say Masturbation is Sin?" at www.ApplyGodsWord.com. Within this article, you will see that masturbation is condemned in the Bible through what is condoned in the Bible.)

8. How can you tell the difference if you are feeling condemned or feeling convicted? What can you do to reject false feelings of condemnation while being careful not to ignore the Holy Spirit's conviction?

The difference between the Holy Spirit's conviction and condemnation is that one makes you feel like you are dead while the other makes you want to pursue life. When you are getting hit with feelings of condemnation, you will feel hopeless, punished, and unloved. Conviction will make you feel honest about your sin, it will lead to you confess and repent, it will make you want to rely on God's grace for redemption, and it will make you move towards God rather that sit still in guilt or fear.

2 Corinthians 7:10, "For godly grief produces a repentance that leads to salvation without regret, whereas worldly grief produces death." Notice that "godly grief produces repentance." This means that when God brings conviction, it will cause a desire to move towards Christ. When you are getting hit with a satanic attack of condemnation or feeling an unholy sorrow for your lustful sins, you will want to sit still and just die. If you're not a Christian, you should feel condemned because you are. The only way to escape condemnation is through being born again through Jesus Christ. Once you are a Christian, you should never feel condemned, "There is therefore now no condemnation for those who are in Christ Jesus" (Romans 8:1). You should only feel conviction.

Always remember that if you rely on God's grace, he always completely wipes away our sins. Psalm 103:11-12, "For as high as the heavens are above the earth, so great is his steadfast love toward those who fear him; as far as the east is from the west, so far does he remove our transgressions from us."

9. We all struggle to read God's word at certain times in life. To help bring motivation, list 10 benefits of regularly reading the Bible.

If you don't see the benefits of knowing God's word, you won't read, study, and memorize it. There are countless reasons to read the word: Correction, wisdom, counsel, conviction, fellowship over it with other believers, it will teach you about God, it will teach you about yourself, it will teach you about believers, it will teach you about unbelievers, it will benefit your marriage, it will help you be a better mom or dad, it will give you financial wisdom, it will help you make wise decisions, it will feed your soul, it will keep you from getting sucked into the world's lies, and so much more.

If you are struggling to come up with the benefits of taking the Scriptures into your heart and mind, read through Psalm 119.

10. No matter where you are at with receiving the Holy Spirit's conviction, we can always be more sensitive to his leading. Write out a prayer asking the Holy Spirit to bring a holy conviction over your sexual sin.

Never grow complacent. There is always a temptation to sin no matter how mature you become. Never let down your guard. Pray to the Lord about what has been tempting you lately or what could be a temptation. Ask him for the strength, desire, and courage to reject evil and pursue God. Tell him how much you love him and how much you know he loves you. Explain why you want to be sexually pure. Pour out your heart. Don't hold back. Don't waist this opportunity to connect with your Heavenly Father. He wants you to talk with him. He wants to help you and show you his love. Your Father loves you.

Going Deeper Chapter 3

1. How does knowing your sexual sin is actually against God help you overcome sexual temptation?

God is the most powerful person in the universe. He has the ability to bless and to take away blessings. I for one want to obey God. Additionally, knowing that all sin is directly connected to our relationship with God helps me find the right solution. Since sin is when we disobey God, the obvious way not to sin is to obey God. I will only obey God if I spend time with him, learn from him, and gain power from him.

2. What's the difference between a mistake and a sin?

The difference is that a mistake was done unintentionally and it was an error that did not break God's commandments. Mistakes are committed against other humans and relate to earthly matters. A sin is against God. It can be against God and humans, but you cannot sin against a human without also sinning against God.

3. Why did the sinful woman in Luke 7:36-50 love Jesus so passionately while the Pharisee loved Jesus so little?

It's clear that the woman knew she was a great sinner in need of a great savior. She loved Jesus so much because she knew that her sin was against God and that Jesus is the Son of God (meaning he is God himself, second in the Trinity). She knew that when he forgave her, he cleared the debt that was against him.

The Pharisee didn't believe any of these things about himself or about Jesus. He didn't believe that he was a great sinner, thus he was not looking for a great savior. He didn't believe he had a debt against God, he didn't believe that Jesus was the Son of God, thus he did not seek Jesus' grace nor had any appreciation for the gift of salvation Jesus alone could give.

4. We all struggle at times to love Jesus as passionately as we would hope. What might some causes be of our lack of passion for pursuing Jesus?

Sin, ultimately, is the root problem to our lack of desire for God. However, sin manifests itself in countless ways. Pride is probably one of the most common ways sin is expressed though humans. Pride is blind to itself, which is why none of us can fully appreciate how lost and hopeless we are without Jesus Christ. The more deeply you understand human depravity compared to God's holiness, the greater you will appreciate and love Jesus for his saving work.

Other causes of a lack of love for Jesus might include idolatry of other gods like sex, lust, porn, masturbation, or a sinful dating lifestyle. The human heart was created to pursue and worship. If we are not pursuing and worshipping God, our hearts will find another god to take God's rightful place. To love Jesus we also need to not love worldly idols.

Another common reason for a lack of love for Jesus is rooted in laziness. Relationships take work. God gives us a relationship with him through grace, but this does not mean we won't have to put forth effort. Works done to gain salvation, grace, or favor is not biblical. But to fully mature and take advantage of the many free blessings God has given us, we will need to work, train, and put forth massive amounts of effort. Sometimes we are not passionate about Jesus because we have not spent the energy necessary to cultivate that passion. Reading your Bible, prayer, fasting, and fellowshipping with other believers all help us stay passionate about Jesus; but all of these good things require us to put forth real effort too.

5. In 2 Samuel 12:9, Nathan, who represents the word of God, says to David, "Why have you despised the word of the LORD, to do what is evil in his sight?" How does spending time in the Bible help us hold onto the truth, resist temptation, and realize that everything revolves around God, including our sin?

King David clearly understood what Nathan was saying, for Psalm 51:4 is really expressing the same truth found in 2 Samuel 12:9. Nathan didn't say, "How could you despise your loyal servant, Uriah, like this?" He didn't say, "How could you be such a poor king to your people and such a poor leader to Bathsheba?" Nathan said, "Why have you despised the word of the Lord, to do what is evil in his sight?" King David spent time hearing God's word and reflecting on it, thus when he writes Psalm 51:4 God's truth came pouring out of him.

Likewise, the more time we spend in the Bible, the more God's truth will come pouring out of us. His truth will keep us from sin and his truth will help us return to him once we do sin.

The world, the flesh, and the devil want to make us believe that everything should revolve around ourselves. When we read and take God's truth into our hearts and minds, it recalibrates us to reality. We can live like God is not at the center of everything, but that's not reality. God will judge us based upon reality. Like it or not, every decision we make is either for or against God. There are no neutral places on this planet. God is at the center of everything. Everything truly is about him. The Bible helps us realize this and overcome the lies we are constantly being fed.

6. What similarities do you see between Acts 9:4 and Psalm 51:4?

Acts 9:1-5 states, "But Saul, still breathing threats and murder against the disciples of the Lord, went to the high priest [2] and asked him for letters to the synagogues at Damascus, so that if he found any belonging to the Way, men or women, he might bring them bound to Jerusalem. [3] Now as he went on his way, he approached Damascus, and suddenly a light from heaven shone around him. [4] And falling to the ground he heard a voice saying to him, "Saul, Saul, why are you persecuting me?" [5] And he said, "Who are you, Lord?" And he said, "I am Jesus, whom you are persecuting."

In Acts 9:1 it says Saul (who was to be named Paul) was persecuting the disciples of the Lord, but then Jesus confronts Saul and says, "Why are you persecuting me?" This is the same truth expressed in Psalm 51:4. Clearly David sinned against many people, but ultimately his sin was against God.

7. How can the death of one man, Jesus, wash away all the sins of those who receive God's grace?

If all sin is against God, then it seems only right that God has the authority to pay for that sin himself if he chooses. No one else has the right to except a different payment for sin. Every sinner deserves to pay for their own sin according to the law. But since the sin is against God, he has the right to accept a different form of payment.

Additionally, the sacrifice of Jesus was great enough to cover every sin ever committed because he is not just a man but he is fully God as well. This is why the doctrine of the Trinity is so important. If Jesus was not fully God and fully man, than his sacrifice would have been left wanting. Jesus was born through a perfect birth, he lived a perfect life, he died a perfect death, and he was raised from the dead all because he was not just a man – he is the Son of God, fully God and fully man.

Hebrews 10:9-14, "[God] does away with the first in order to establish the second. [10] And by that will we have been sanctified through the offering of the body of Jesus Christ once for all. [11] And every priest stands daily at his service, offering repeatedly the same sacrifices, which can never take away sins. [12] But when Christ had offered for all time a single sacrifice for sins, he sat down at the right hand of God, [13] waiting from that time until his enemies should be made a footstool for his feet. [14] For by a single offering he has perfected for all time those who are being sanctified."

8. What reasons do you want to overcome sexual sin? While these reasons may be good, do you think these reasons will always motivate you? Why or why not?

There are many good motives that we should have when it comes to overcoming sexual temptation. It is good to want to stop sinning sexually for the sake of your wife, your kids, your family, your societal impact, your own well being, and so many other reasons. However, all of these motives are not the best motive. Those we love will eventually do something to hurt us. While we will forgive them, in our moments of hurt we will be susceptible to sexual temptation and sin. Kids grow up, spouses have bad days, society will tick you off, and you won't always care about your own well being.

God alone is the one who will never leave us nor forsake us (Hebrews 13:5). God alone will be the one who can provide the motivation to resist sexual temptation. God should be our ultimate motivation for all the good that we do. He's God, we are to glorify him above everything else, and we will not be satisfied until we fulfill this calling/design on our life.

Colossians 3:17, "And whatever you do, in word or deed, do everything in the name of the Lord Jesus, giving thanks to God the Father through him." If you were to keep reading, Paul then *gives instructions on how to love as wives, husbands, children, and slaves/employees through Colossians 3:18-25. While we must love others and treat them with the respect they deserve, our foundational motive must be to glorify God.*

9. What is your general understanding of the glory of God? How would you define it? How can Christians glorify God?

The glory of God is one of the most important subjects within the entire Bible. God does everything for his own glory. Humans and all of creation were made to glorify God. So often, however, we don't really understand what the glory of God is and how Christians are to glorify God.

The "glory of God" and "glorify God" are used in multiple ways throughout Scripture. So boiling down one specific definition is difficult. However, most often the glory of God refers to the invisible qualities of God made visible. This is why Jesus Christ glorifies God the most because he reveals the most about God. Jesus visibly shows us the qualities of the invisible God (Colossians 1:15).

Hebrews 1:1-3, "Long ago, at many times and in many ways, God spoke to our fathers by the prophets, [2] but in these last days he has spoken to us by his Son, whom he appointed the heir of all things, through whom also he created the world. [3] He is the radiance of the glory of God and the exact imprint of his nature, and he upholds the universe by the word of his power."

God use to make himself known through the prophets, but now he has made himself known more fully through Jesus who is fully God and fully man. In short, you can say the Jesus is the glory of God and the way we glorify God is by imitating Christ and living like him.

10. How does sex between a man and woman glorify (reflect) God? Why does sexual sin not glorify God?

Within sex as God intended it, between a married man and woman, there is an abundance of symbolism that is to reflect God. Sex is to be between one man and one woman who are *committed to each other for their entire life. God commits to his people forever.*

According to Ephesians 5:22-33, marriage, which includes sex, is suppose to represent Christ and his Church. In marriage the husband is to represent Christ and the wife is supposed to represent the Church. The husband is to be the leader and initiator within the marriage because Christ is this within his marriage to the Church. Not to be too graphic, but within sex, if the man does not initiate and "rise to the occasion" nothing is going to happen. The wife must be vulnerable and "receive" her husband, just as the Church must also respond to and receive the leadership of God. Leadership and submission in marriage reflects the leadership of Christ and the submission of all Christians (male and female) to Christ.

Marriage also reflects God because within marriage there is equal value between husband and wife but there are clearly different roles. Within the Trinity, this is true as well. Each member of the Trinity, Father, Son, and Holy Spirit, are fully God. Yet each is distinct from one another and fulfills different roles with their relationship.

There are endlessly more ways sex and marriage reflect (glorify) God.

Going Deeper Chapter 4

1. Do you believe that people are born sinful or that they sin and then become sinful? Why do you believe this?

I believe that people are born sinful and then they express this by sinning. I believe this because the Scriptures point to this fact (Psalm 51:5, Romans 5:12). Every human besides Jesus Christ, in theological terms, is "fully depraved." Theologically, this does not mean that we have all sinned the same amount or that we have all sinned as much as could have. "Fully depraved" does not mean that we have sinned to our fullest potential but that every part of us has been infected with sin. No part of a human is left unaffected by sin.

Another theological term that is important to this topic is "original sin." This term means that Adam and Eve committed the first sin and now every human who is their offspring has inherited from birth their sinfulness. This is one reason the virgin birth of Jesus is so important. He stopped the chain of sinful events through human history because he did not come to earth through human means. Thank God for the gospel!

Romans 5:18-20, "Consequently, just as one trespass resulted in condemnation for all people, so also one righteous act resulted in justification and life for all people. [19] For just as through the disobedience of the one man the many were made sinners, so also through the obedience of the one man the many will be made righteous."

2. How do solutions look different when we seek to treat the external problems compared to treating the internal problems? Do you agree that an internal problem needs an internal solution?

When we seek to treat the external problems, we often blame our circumstances or our environment rather than our sinful nature. The world only looks to deal with external solutions because they do not understand that all of us are sinful without Jesus Christ. This false belief that every problem is because of our external environments or biological makeup has even crept into our judicial system. So often people are given a lesser punishment for their crimes because our society seeks to blame something other than the individual for the people's individual sinful choices.

I do believe that at an internal problem needs an internal solution. The heart is the issue, no amount of external solutions will help. This is not to devalue the importance of external helps, but it is simply meant as a warning against putting your hope in some solution other than Jesus Christ.

3. If you struggle with pornography, have you tried to use porn blockers or some other external solution? What happened? What are the pros and cons to external solutions to sexual sin?

Porn blockers are good. No one should be scoffed at who seeks to use such precautions. With that said, porn blockers will not stop you from lusting after pornography if you are not addressing the issues of your heart. People are smart. When their sinful nature is raging, they can easily find other means to sin. Sexual sin was around before the internet, live streaming, DVD, VHS, magazines, and all the other means before these. The problem is not with the means. The internet can be used for good or bad depending on the person who is using it.

My experience with porn blockers is that they only work when people use them as a result of a changed heart. If you seek to use external solutions as the cause and catalyst for change and transformation, you are sure to fail. Porn blockers and other such precautions are good and can help us in moments of weakness. They give you that extra time you need to really process what you are about to do. But if you heart is not right with God through Jesus Christ, nothing is going to stop your lustful sin.

4. Why do you think porn use is so prevalent these days?

I think porn use is so prevalent because of its ease and accessibility. Before the internet, you had to be a lot bolder to use porn. You had to go get it or order it to your house. Now It's just as easy to look at porn as it is to make a phone call. Simply pull out your smart phone and in literally under 10 seconds you can view porn. It's as if we are all carrying around little porn shops in our pockets.

Obviously smart phones, tablets, and online access are not the real problem. These tools are used and wonderful too. I love having a smart phone because it's also like having a huge Christian library in your pocket. When I want to remember a Bible verse but I can only think of a few words, I can simply search those few key words and usually my search results will come back with the full Bible verse.

Porn use is also so prevalent because of how secular our American culture has become. The more we have removed God form our daily lives as a nation, the more our nation loses self-control. A society is the sum of our individual choices. Throughout America, people are becoming less and less Christ-like. Thus sins, like lusting over porn, have become more prevalent throughout our society.

5. What internal feelings and emotions do you have when you are most tempted by sexual sins? Do you see any relationship between your internal feelings and what you are sexually attracted to?

This question is worth spending some time in prayer over. What types of fantasies are you drawn to? When your fleshly desires are out of control, do they express themselves through desiring to dominant or be dominated? Are you attracted to older women, younger women, or people of the same sex? Questions like these can be unconformable, but they are necessary to answer if you hope to better identify the root issues.

For example, gay men often have an internal longing for male attention they never received as children from their fathers. The problem is that they have sexualized these feelings and thus they are tempted to live a homosexual lifestyle. Some men are attracted to younger women because they are afraid of women their age. Some women are attracted to older men because they associate these men with financial stability. If these women, for example, dealt with their money issues, their desire for older men would be under control as well. People who struggle with anger often times are drawn to the type of porn which depicts violent scenes. If the anger was solved, the temptation to watch degrading porn would lose its power.

The point is, so often are sexual desires are tied to other undealt with issues. To stop falling to sexual temptation, sometimes we have to deal with issues that seem completely unrelated.

6. What's the difference between godly sorrow and worldly sorrow (2 Corinthians 7:10)?

2 Corinthians 7:8-11, "Even if I caused you sorrow by my letter, I do not regret it. Though I did regret it—I see that my letter hurt you, but only for a little while—[9] yet now I am happy, not because you were made sorry, but because your sorrow led you to repentance. For you became sorrowful as God intended and so were not harmed in any way by us. [10] Godly sorrow brings repentance that leads to salvation and leaves no regret, but worldly sorrow brings death. [11] See what this godly sorrow has produced in you: what earnestness, what eagerness to clear yourselves, what indignation, what alarm, what longing, what concern, what readiness to see justice done."

As you study the Bible verses above, it's clear that worldly sorrow terminates on itself. In other words, worldly sorrow ends with worldly sorrow and death. You're not moving forward in this type of sorrow. Godly sorrow, however, "brings repentance that leads to salvation and leaves no regret." In other words, godly sorrow does not end in godly sorrow. Godly sorrow moves you forward towards God. Your grief and sadness over your sin causes you to repent and run back to your heavenly Father. Godly sorrow and worldly sorrow may look similar in the beginning, but you will be able to decipher the two by the fruit they are producing in your life. Worldly sorrow produces death, godly sorrow produces repentance which leads to life.

7. Some people use their sin nature as an excuse, "Well, I can't help myself, I am sinful after all. Thank God for forgiveness though. . . ." But then they keep sinning and don't truly repent. How does David's realization of his sinful nature help him choose the right road to truly repent?

Most men I've talked to have experienced a temptation based in this logic, "Oh what the heck, I've already started to sin now

*. . . I'll just binge sin for a little while before I repent to God."
Or they say something like, "I just can't help myself. The Bible
says I am sinful. I know God is going to forgive me anyway, so
who cares if I keep sinning."*

*David doesn't use his sinful nature as an excuse. His realization
of his sin nature only magnifies his remorse. Because he knows
he's flawed, he knows he must rely on God for the real
solution. David doesn't see is flaws as an excuse to sin more,
he sees his flaws as the reasons he is so desperately in need of
a great Savior.*

*Likewise, David didn't use God's abundant love, grace, and
mercy as justification to sin. He believed God would forgive
him, which did not make him want to sin more but rather it
drew him to God even more. He knew God would forgive, so
this brought David back to God. The fact that he knew God
would forgive did not draw him to sin more.*

*If we have a wrong response to God's grace, this may mean
that we are not truly saved. When you truly receive God's
grace, you will not have a consistent desire to abuse it. You will
need God's grace desperately throughout your whole life, but
when you are truly a Christian you will not take God's mercy
for granted. His lavish love will draw you to himself and away
from sin, and if does otherwise you are not living in Christ.*

**8. Do you think there is a connection between our passion
for Jesus and our personal realization for our own sinfulness
apart from Jesus? If we don't think our condition is that bad
apart from Christ, do you think this affects our desire to
pursue Christ?**

*We are far worse off without Christ than we realize, and we
are far better off with Christ than we realize. We don't fully*

comprehend how sinful we really are without Jesus, and we don't fully realize how righteous we have become because of Jesus when we are saved by him. The more deeply we come to grips with both of these sides of the coin, the greater we will love, appreciate, and pursue Jesus.

9. C.S. Lewis said, "No man knows how bad he is till he has tried very hard to be good." Have you tried very hard to be good in your own power? What was the result?

During the years where I was living in sexual sin, I remember often times making promises to God in my youth. I would set dates, promising that after such and such a date, I would completely stop 100% of my sexual sin. I would promise right after my sin that I would never do that again. In all of these instances my desire was good by my approach was unwise.

I was a Christian who was struggling with sexual temptation. Therefore I felt guilty when I sinned. I tried very, very hard to be good. The result was always the same: failure. In fact, it seemed like the harder I tried to resist in my own power, the faster I fell.

Romans 7:14-25, " We know that the law is spiritual; but I am unspiritual, sold as a slave to sin. ^{15} I do not understand what I do. For what I want to do I do not do, but what I hate I do. ^{16} And if I do what I do not want to do, I agree that the law is good. ^{17} As it is, it is no longer I myself who do it, but it is sin living in me. ^{18} For I know that good itself does not dwell in me, that is, in my sinful nature.[c] For I have the desire to do what is good, but I cannot carry it out. ^{19} For I do not do the good I want to do, but the evil I do not want to do—this I keep on *doing. ²⁰ Now if I do what I do not want to do, it is no longer I who do it, but it is sin living in me that does it.*

²¹ So I find this law at work: Although I want to do good, evil is right there with me. ²² For in my inner being I delight in God's law; ²³ but I see another law at work in me, waging war against the law of my mind and making me a prisoner of the law of sin at work within me. ²⁴ What a wretched man I am! Who will rescue me from this body that is subject to death? ²⁵ Thanks be to God, who delivers me through Jesus Christ our Lord!

10. Read about Judas in Matthew 27:1-10. Why did Judas kill himself? How can we avoid denying our sin or being overwhelmed by our sin?

Judas is an example of someone who felt worldly sorrow and not godly sorrow. Of the three options when confronted with our own sinfulness that were talked about in this chapter (denial, suicide, or repentance) Judas was now no longer able to deny his depravity, and since he did not do the right thing and repent, he took the only option left – suicide. Once he finally came to his senses and realized how wickedly he acted, he was completely overwhelmed by the gravity of his rebellion. Judas is a microcosm of every sinner who does not repent. We can deny our sinfulness, run from it through death, but we cannot live with the full weight of it. Without Jesus there is no hope. Thankfully we do have Jesus, thus we do have a very great hope in him.

Going Deeper Chapter 5

1. When you think about Jesus' crucifixion, what benefits do you associate with this?

The most common benefit associated with the cross is the forgiveness of sins. However, throughout the pages of Scripture, there are many benefits to the cross. Certainly we should celebrate our forgiveness. These statements of mine are not meant to devalue our forgiveness in any way. My intention is the opposite. Because of the great sacrifice of Jesus Christ on the cross, I would hate for us to miss out on all that God intends for us to enjoy.

For example: Colossians 2:13-15, "And you, who were dead in your trespasses and the uncircumcision of your flesh, God made alive together with him, having forgiven us all our trespasses, [14] by canceling the record of debt that stood against us with its legal demands. This he set aside, nailing it to the cross. [15] He disarmed the rulers and authorities and put them to open shame, by triumphing over them in him."

Here we can see that not only are we forgiven, but "He disarmed the rulers and authorities and put them to open shame, by triumphing over them in him." Satan no longer has any hold on us because of the cross of Christ!

2. What is justification and sanctification? How do these two terms relate to one another?

Excerpt from Chapter 5:

"Justification is the legal transaction of God who puts the qualities of Christ onto you. When God looks at Christians, he sees the perfections of Christ. He doesn't just look at us this way to be kind, like a naive parent who thinks there little devil is an angel. God always sees the absolute truth. The power of the cross is real.

We all know, however, we don't live a perfect life once we become a Christian. While all Christians are objectively and positionally fully justified in Christ, we are all also being sanctified. The process of sanctification is where you learn to live out who you already are in Christ. This is where the rubber meets the road. And the way sanctification happens is through active faith in your justification.

Justification is something that is done to you; sanctification requires your active participation. When you are justified, God puts Christ's righteousness on you. Sanctification occurs when you participate with the Holy Spirit's leading and you start to live out the righteousness God has given you. The more deeply you believe and trust who you truly are in Christ, the more this will manifest in your day-to-day life. The more you believe in God's justification of you, the more you will experience his sanctification in you"

3. Do you think there is a difference between belief and trust? How is "believing" you are a new creation in Christ different than actively "trusting" this?

You can believe that the airplane is safe to fly in. But until you get in and let the pilot take you for a ride, you do not trust this fact. You can believe your spouse is honest with the finances, but you do not trust him or her until you stop checking the credit card statements twice a day and once before you go to bed at night. You can believe God will take care of you, but you do not trust this until you stop worrying.

Belief is important. It is the intellectual acceptance of facts. Christianity does include this. Trust is where the rubber meets the road. When you trust the facts about Christianity, this will be shown in your transformed/changed life. You can believe Christianity without being a Christian. Once you trust Christ and your life is transformed, this is the evidence that you are truly a Christian. To say this in more biblical language, "faith" is belief and trust in God.

4. How does your thought life relate to your actions?

Actions are birthed in the mind. Romans 13:13-14 (NIV), "Let us behave decently, as in the daytime, not in carousing and drunkenness, not in sexual immorality and debauchery, not in dissension and jealousy. [14] Rather, clothe yourselves with the Lord Jesus Christ, and do not think about how to gratify the desires of the flesh."

Clearly there is a connection between our thoughts and our ability to resist sexual immorality. We must take control of our thought life. It's hard work to control your mind. You have to overcome every false and evil thought with the truth of Scripture. Every time something unhelpful pops into your mind, you need to be armed with God's truth. When you believe and think about truth rather than evil desires, your actions change.

2 Corinthians 10:3-5, "For though we live in the world, we do not wage war as the world does. [4] The weapons we fight with are not the weapons of the world. On the contrary, they have divine power to demolish strongholds. [5] We demolish arguments and every pretension that sets itself up against the knowledge of God, and we take captive every thought to make it obedient to Christ."

5. What are ways you can assure your thought life is healthy and rooted in biblical facts rather than controlled by your human emotions?

One obvious way is to consistently read, study, and memorize the Bible. Without reading large and different chunks of the Bible, we will not have a good understanding of the larger picture God is seeking to show us. Without studying smaller parts of Scripture more in depth, we will not have a deepening knowledge of his truth. Without memorizing parts of the Bible on a regular base, we will not have the truth at our finger tips like we need it.

Memorizing Scripture is probably the hardest to do for most Christians; however, it also the most beneficial. To store God's word in your mind and heart is the best way to ensure that your thoughts are biblically healthy rather than controlled by our human emotions.

Lastly, having honest friends who know the Bible will also keep you from straying from the truth. By talking with those people who love Jesus, who love you, and who know the word of God, they can point out faulty thinking and choices when you need them to help you.

6. Do you believe you have a choice to think about certain things and avoid thinking about other things? In other words, do you believe you can control your mind or does it just control you?

Philippians 4:8, "Finally, brothers, whatever is true, whatever is honorable, whatever is just, whatever is pure, whatever is lovely, whatever is commendable, if there is any excellence, if there is anything worthy of praise, think about these things."

Colossians 3:2, "Set your minds on things that are above, not on things that are on earth."

As much as it may feel that our mind is controlling itself, we do have control of our thought life. The two verses above are just a small sampling of the many Bible verses that command us to control our minds. If we did not have the ability as Christians to control what we think about, God would not command us to guard our thoughts.

If we let our minds wander, our mind will control us. But as Christians, we have to submit to the Holy Spirit and what the Holy Spirit has said in his word, and when we do we will have the ability to control our thoughts.

Romans 8:5-8, "For those who live according to the flesh set their minds on the things of the flesh, but those who live according to the Spirit set their minds on the things of the Spirit. [6] For to set the mind on the flesh is death, but to set the mind on the Spirit is life and peace. [7] For the mind that is set on the flesh is hostile to God, for it does not submit to God's law;

indeed, it cannot. ⁸ Those who are in the flesh cannot please God."

To control our minds we must choose to "live according to the Spirit" for "those who are in the flesh cannot please God."

7. Satan often tries to get us to doubt our transformation, "If you were really changed, then why are you still struggling with porn, masturbation, and lust?" What is the biblical answer to this lie? If we really are a new creation in Christ, why do we still sin?

Philippians 3:12-14, "Not that I have already obtained this or am already perfect, but I press on to make it my own, because Christ Jesus has made me his own. ¹³ Brothers, I do not consider that I have made it my own. But one thing I do: forgetting what lies behind and straining forward to what lies ahead, ¹⁴ I press on toward the goal for the prize of the upward call of God in Christ Jesus."

Hebrews 10:14, "For by a single offering he has perfected for all time those who are being sanctified"

As the Bible verses above indicate, Jesus Christ has given us his perfections but we are also being sanctified. Sanctification is the process of learning, growing, and becoming more and more like Christ. Justification happens at the moment of conversion; sanctification takes place over our lifetime.

The reason you still struggle with sin even though God has transformed you is because you are in the process of learning to live from that transformation. God does not overpower us to make us obedient robots; he empowers us so we can be obedient humans.

8. Read Romans 7:13-25. Summarize these verses in your own words.

Perhaps read Romans 7:13-25 in the Message Translation or the New Living Translation to hear these words in a different way.

God gave us the law to show us how sinful we are. The law didn't make us sinful. Sin, however, sees the law and desire to do the opposite of what it commands.

However, when we become a Christian through the power of the gospel, we have a new desire in us. Sin remains in our body and wants to disobey the law, but now that the Holy Spirit is in us our true selves desire to obey God. Thus we end up doing what we don't want to do. By having this obvious war within ourselves, we can see that there really are now two forces fighting for control. There's the real you, the new man/woman in Christ; but there's also the old sinful nature. The important thing to remember is that you are no longer your old sinful nature. For as Paul painstakingly seeks to make clear, "So now it is no longer I who do it, but sin that dwells within me. For I know that nothing good dwells in me, that is, in my flesh" (Romans 7:17-18).

You can feel how Paul makes every effort to show that there is a difference between him and his flesh.

The only solution to this problem is Jesus Christ. Jesus sanctifies us throughout our life, helping us grow more and more in control. He will finally set us free completely, however, when we are raised from the dead, giving us new bodies, and thus we will no longer struggle with our old sinful nature.

9. Even though the true you is no longer your sinful nature, why is it still absolutely necessary to take responsibility for your sins, confess them to God, and repent? If our sinful nature is responsible for our sins, why are we still to blame?

One of the signs of having a new nature in Christ is that you take responsibility for your old nature. If you deny you are responsible, if you are proud rather than humble, and if you make excuses rather than repent to the Lord, this is evidence that you are not living from the new man, or perhaps you are not saved at all.

On this side of eternity, one of the signs of our salvation is that we recognize our sinfulness, repent, and rely on God's grace.

1 John 1:10, "If we say we have not sinned, we make him a liar, and his word is not in us."

10. List a handful of Bible verses that proclaim the truth about your real identity in Christ. Challenger yourself to memorize some of these so you are ready to believe biblical facts rather than sinful temptations, urges, and feelings.

Galatians 3:26, "So in Christ Jesus you are all children of God through faith."

1 John 3:1, "See what great love the Father has lavished on us, that we should be called children of God! And that is what we are!"

Romans 5:1, "Therefore, since we have been justified through faith, we have peace with God through our Lord Jesus Christ."

Romans 6:4, "We were therefore buried with him through baptism into death in order that, just as Christ was raised from the dead through the glory of the Father, we too may live a new life."

Romans 6:6-7, "For we know that our old self was crucified with him so that the body ruled by sin might be done away with, that we should no longer be slaves to sin— [7] because anyone who has died has been set free from sin."

Ephesians 2:10, "For we are God's workmanship, created in Christ Jesus to do good works, which God prepared in advance for us to do."

Colossians 1:13-14, "For he has rescued us from the dominion of darkness and brought us into the kingdom of the Son he loves, [14] in whom we have redemption, the forgiveness of sins."

Colossians 3:1-3, "Since, then, you have been raised with Christ, set your hearts on things above, where Christ is, seated at the right hand of God. [2] Set your minds on things above, not on earthly things. [3] For you died, and your life is now hidden with Christ in God."

Galatians 2:20, "I have been crucified with Christ and I no longer live, but Christ lives in me. The life I now live in the body, I live by faith in the Son of God, who loved me and gave himself for me."

Galatians 6:14-15, "May I never boast except in the cross of our Lord Jesus Christ, through which the world has been crucified to me, and I to the world. [15] Neither circumcision nor uncircumcision means anything; what counts is the new creation."

2 Corinthians 5:15-17, "And he died for all, that those who live should no longer live for themselves but for him who died for them and was raised again.[16] So from now on we regard no one from a worldly point of view. Though we once regarded Christ in this way, we do so no longer. [17] Therefore, if anyone is in Christ, the new creation has come: The old has gone, the new is here!"

(Romans 8:1-4 ,Romans 8:9-11, Romans 8:15, Ephesians 4:24, Ephesians 2, Ephesians 5:8, Colossians 1:21-23, Colossians 2:9-10, Colossians 3:1-17, Psalm 103:1-5, Psalm 103:12, Psalm 37:23-24, Philippians 2:13, Philippians 3:9, , 1 Corinthians 1:30, 2 Corinthians 3:5-6, 2 Corinthians 5:21, 2 Corinthians 6:18, John 8:36, 1 Peter 2:9)

Going Deeper Chapter 6

1. Jesus did not die and rise from the dead so you could feel sorry about your sin forever. Jesus died and rose so you could be transformed. What does the resurrection of Jesus Christ accomplish for the Christian?

Romans 6:4-11, "We were buried therefore with him by baptism into death, in order that, just as Christ was raised from the dead by the glory of the Father, we too might walk in newness of life. For if we have been united with him in a death like his, we shall certainly be united with him in a resurrection like his. ⁶ We know that our old self was crucified with him in order that the body of sin might be brought to nothing, so that we would no longer be enslaved to sin. ⁷ For one who has died has been set free from sin. ⁸ Now if we have died with Christ, we believe that we will also live with him. ⁹ We know that Christ, being raised from the dead, will never die again; death no longer has dominion over him. ¹⁰ For the death he died he died to sin, once for all, but the life he lives he lives to God. ¹¹ So you also must consider yourselves dead to sin and alive to God in Christ Jesus."

The resurrection of Christ is what brings us new life. We need to die with Christ through the cross, but we also need to be raised to new life with Christ through the resurrection. If you only study and understand the cross, you are missing out on life. Jesus' resurrection made us "alive to God in Christ Jesus."

2. Consider Psalm 51:10 in the light of Matthew 15:19. Do you think it is crucial that solutions to sexual sin must address the issues of the heart? Why or Why not?

Matthew 5:19, "For out of the heart come evil thoughts, murder, adultery, sexual immorality, theft, false witness, slander."

The source of our sexual sin does not need to be mysterious. While I encourage you to get counseling, look at your childhood, and even explore helpful psychological principles which don't contradict Scripture, I also caution you not to over complicate things.

While your sexual behavior certainly is directly connected to the environment that you have grown up in and currently live in, the real issue is universally the same for every human – the human heart. As you've probably heard before, "The heart of the problem is the problem of the heart."

Therefore, while dissecting your past and using external solutions (pornography internet blockers, accountability partners, physiological techniques, est.) are certainly not wrong, you are basically wasting your time if you are not willing to address your heart through the power of Jesus Christ. Once you become a Christian, your heart is no longer bad. The real you has a new heart (Ezekiel 36:26), and from that heart you must seek to live if you hope to please the Lord and reject sexual temptation.

3. Revisit what sexual sins you specifically desire to resist? How's it going thus far since you started this study? What are you going to pursue in place of what you seek to avoid?

Just be honest with yourself and God. If you are the small group leader, use wisdom on how to approach this question. If you and your group have built a solid foundation of friendship, feel free to open this up for those who would want to share. I recommend you don't force people to share if they don't volunteer. Let people make the decision on how much they want to share about the specifics of their sexual struggles.

However, there is great value in being specific. 1 John 1:5-7, "God is light, and in him is no darkness at all. ⁶ If we say we have fellowship with him while we walk in darkness, we lie and do not practice the truth. ⁷ But if we walk in the light, as he is in the light, we have fellowship with one another, and the blood of Jesus his Son cleanses us from all sin."

If we want to have fellowship with God and other Christians, we must bring everything into the light. Name your sin specifically. Confess your sins to God in detail.

Secondly, pray specifically about what you want instead of your sexual sin. Pursue intimacy with your Father, satisfaction in Christ, joy in the Holy Spirit, fellowship with your spouse, and freedom to obey God rather than your sin. It's not enough to avoid what you hate. You need to pursue what you love.

The Bible is full of motivational promises. God tells us about the rewards he grants because he knows it will help us pursue him. As Jesus said, "And your Father who sees in secret will reward you" (Matthew 6:4)

4. Why did God not stop us when we sinned in the past?

It's right to wish that we did not rebel against God in our pasts. However, to feel hopeless and that the only solution would have been for God to stop your sin is simply unbiblical. God didn't stop us from our lusts of the past because he didn't have to. The gospel of Jesus Christ is more than enough to make right what went wrong. When we just wish that God would have stopped us from sinning like we did, we are devaluing the sacrifice of Jesus Christ on our behalf.

God also did not stop our sin because he made us human, and to be human we must be free to choose. Without choice there is no real love. While God certainly does elect and preordain our futures, this does not contradict the fact that God also gives humans the freedom to make real choices with real consequences. Our human minds may not be able to fully understand how these two truths can coexist, but that's okay. God understands it and God has made it this way.

When Charles Spurgeon was asked about how he reconciles the sovereignty of God and man's free will, he brilliantly stated, "I do not try to reconcile friends."

5. Compare 2 Samuel 12:15 and 2 Samuel 12:24. What sticks out to you about the different words used in these verses?

2 Samuel 12:15, "And the Lord afflicted the child that Uriah's wife bore to David, and he became sick."

2 Samuel 12:24, "Then David comforted his wife, Bathsheba, and went in to her and lay with her, and she bore a son, and he called his name Solomon."

I find it interesting and noteworthy that Bathsheba is referred to as Uriah's wife, but then she is referred to as David's wife. Sadly, God allowed the baby to die to show his displeasure over sin. When Solomon is born, however, God can bless their children because God has redeemed this situation through his grace, which is highlighted in how he no longer refers to Bathsheba as Uriah's wife. God made the whole situation new, he redeemed Bathsheba and David, and thus they are no longer identified by their former life.

(As a side note, I think it's worth pointing out that the death of their firstborn child together seems to be a foreshadowing of the death of Jesus Christ. The first born needed to pay for the sins committed. Just as God killed the first born Egyptian males in the exodus out of Egypt, just as God told Abraham to sacrifice his first born son (but then stopped him), and just as many other sacrifices were to be the first born male animals — God was setting the stage for Jesus Christ. Jesus Christ was the ultimate first- born-Son-sacrifice who paid for the sins of the whole world.)

6. What were you taught growing up about sexual purity? How did this negatively or positively affect you?

As a young man I was taught that you could lose your purity. I'm grateful to those youth pastors who sought to sow truth into me, but most of the time their tactic to help me behave well was to pressure me with the fear of consequences. These tactics were effective to some degree, but no amount of fear is able to overpower the lusts of a young man who is not walking closely with Jesus.

Therefore, while there were some positive effects, the negative effects were that I felt an overwhelming shame/condemnation when I did sinned. This shame was not a healthy conviction of the Holy Spirit, but a human fear that I had blown it in such a way that God could not redeem me.

Additionally, I also began to idolize the sexual purity of women. Because I felt sexual purity was something you could only retain from birth, I was petrified of falling in love with someone who had somehow blown it just as badly as me. I needed someone else to be the perfect person I was not.

Jesus had to break these lies in me. He revealed to me that I was looking for a woman to be my "perfect one." I was so desperate for a perfect woman because I did not have Jesus Christ as I needed him. Jesus Christ is the perfect One we are all looking for. If we don't have him or if we are devaluing him in our life, we will try to make other people our savior.

Once I was satisfied in Christ and understood that he actually transfers his perfections onto us, only then was I set free to find my wife (who wasn't perfect because no human is perfect) and love her without putting the pressure on her to be my Savior.

7. If you can't lose your newness in Christ, what can happen to you when you sin? What are the consequences of sexual sin for a Christian?

Despite the biblical fact that a true Christian cannot lose his or her salvation, this does not mean ours sins do not have real consequences. If you are a real Christian living in sin, your life will have to be miserable. If you claim to be a Christian and yet you are happily living in sin with no intention or desire to repent, then you are not a real Christian.

A real Christian who is struggling with addictive, chronic sins like lust, masturbation, or pornography will feel horrible about this. Therefore, one of the consequences for a Christian who repeatedly falls to sexual temptation is a lack of joy. You are still God's son or daughter, but when we run from him our relationship suffers. So although your salvation cannot be lost, your joyful experience of your salvation can be lost. Surely this is why King David prayed, "Restore to me the joy of your salvation" (Psalm 51:12).

8. Is the human heart good or bad? (Read Jeremiah 17:9 and Ezekiel 36:26-27)

Jeremiah 17:9, "The heart is deceitful above all things, and desperately sick; who can understand it?"

Ezekiel 36:26-27, "And I will give you a new heart, and a new spirit I will put within you. And I will remove the heart of stone from your flesh and give you a heart of flesh. [27] And I will put my Spirit within you, and cause you to walk in my statutes and be careful to obey my rules.

Put simply, without Jesus Christ and his gospel, the human heart remains deceitfully wicked. However, the sinful heart is why Jesus came. Jesus would not forgive us of our sins but then leave us with no solution to the root problem, doomed to live endlessly with no hope of pleasing him.

So often people quote Jeremiah 17:9 as though this is the Christian's current condition. You need to read the rest of the book, for in Jeremiah 31:33, God explains his new covenant, "For this is the covenant that I will make with the house of Israel after those days, declares the Lord: I will put my law within them, and I will write it on their hearts. And I will be their God, and they shall be my people." God wouldn't write his law on our old hearts. God gives us new hearts because our old hearts were so twisted with sin.

9. If the newness of Christ can never be taken away from a Christian, does this fact tempt us to sin more? What should be our reaction to learning that Christ's perfections can never be taken away from us? (Read Romans 6:1-4)

Romans 6:1-4, "What shall we say then? Are we to continue in sin that grace may abound? [2] By no means! How can we who died to sin still live in it? [3] Do you not know that all of us who have been baptized into Christ Jesus were baptized into his death? [4] We were buried therefore with him by baptism into death, in order that, just as Christ was raised from the dead by the glory of the Father, we too might walk in newness of life."

Paul's explanation of God's grace and justification through Romans 1-5 was so lavish, he knew that people would think that he was saying that sinning didn't matter. For at the very end of Romans 5 just before Romans 6:1-4, Paul states, ". . . where sin increased, grace abounded all the more . . . ." This is quite the statement! It seems that there is literally no sin great enough to outweigh the grace of God.

The obvious temptation, therefore, is to become lax in our resistance to sin. "If God will forgive me anyways, then who cares if I give into lust and sexual temptations?" Paul explains in Romans 6:1-4 that the reason statements like these don't apply is because a true Christian would never say this as a continual reason to rebel. You may be tempted now and then with this faulty thinking, but if this is your regular explanation for sin, then you must take Paul's question to heart, "How can we who died to sin live in it?"

God's abundant grace is not the reason you can sin as much as you want and not repent, it is the reason why no matter how much you struggle with sin, you can always repent and seek his forgiveness.

10. If someone asked you why you wanted to overcome sexual temptation, how would you answer?

I know we've already talked about how the only lasting motives will be those motives rooted in a desire to love and glorify God. However, when we love and glorify God, we will express this in specific and practical ways. The way you love God is most often expressed in how you love other people, in the lifestyle you choose to live, and in the missions you fight for.

So don't feel the need to be overly theological with this question. Just be honest. If you're struggling to answer this, ask yourself this question, "If you woke up tomorrow and all *your problems regarding sexual sin completely vanished, what would be different?" By imagining what your life and relationships would be like without the guilt and negative consequences of sexual sin, you can then better picture the reason you are fighting this battle.*

Going Deeper Chapter 7

1. Do you believe you can lose your salvation? Why or why not?

I do not believe you can lose your salvation because the Bible does not state that you can.

John 10:28-29, "I give them eternal life, and they will never perish, and no one will snatch them out of my hand. My Father, who has given them to me, is greater than all, and no one is able to snatch them out of the Father's hand."

John 6:37, "All that the Father gives me will come to me, and whoever comes to me I will never cast out."

Romans 11:29, "For the gifts and the calling of God are irrevocable."

However, the Bible does point to the reality that many people think they are saved when they are really not. We will witness people in our lives that we thought were saved but then seem to "lose their salvation." The Bible explains this situation differently. Rather than losing their salvation, the Scriptures state that people like this were never truly saved to begin with.

1 John 2:19, "They went out from us, but they were not of us; for if they had been of us, they would have continued with us. But they went out, that it might become plain that they all are not of us."

Eternal security is often abused because people feel they can just do whatever they want and still go to heaven. The problem with this thinking is that if you were truly saved, you would have a desire to obey God. Eternal security should be a comfort to the genuine Christian who repents of sin. We need not fear that God will abandon us. This doctrine should not be abused, however; for it you abuse it, it probably doesn't apply to you since you most likely are not actually saved if you live in sin and don't repent.

2. Why do you think King David prayed Psalm 51:11?

There are many reasons I believe King David prayed Psalm 51:11. One reason I don't believe he prayed it was that he was afraid of losing his salvation. In the Old Testament, the full picture of Christian salvation was not yet completely revealed. Those in the Old Testament like King David, though, were still only saved through the gospel of Jesus Christ (Romans 3:23-26). As you read through passages of Scripture like Romans 3-4, God explains that people's obedience in the Old Testament was their expression of faith in God. Thus people were saved through faith and not good works even before Jesus came and revealed his gospel.

David probably understood the Holy Spirit in the context of dwelling on him rather than in him. People were anointed by the Holy Spirit then but the Holy Spirit had not come fully to dwell within Christians until the book of Acts.

3. Read Galatians 5:16-26. How does this passage of Scripture help us overcome sexual temptation?

This passage of Scripture explains the real problem causing our lusts and desire for sexual sins. It also explains the solution to sexual temptation and all forms of sexual immorality. In short, if we obey our flesh/sinful nature, we will produce the fruits of the flesh. If we are led by the Spirit, then we will produce the fruits of the Spirit. One of the fruits of the Spirit is self-control. If you want to have control of yourself, you need to submit to the control of the Holy Spirit. He does not possess us and turn us into mindless slaves. Rather, when we are being led by the Spirit, he frees us from having to obey the lustful desires of our flesh.

As Bob Dylan sang, "You're gonna have to serve somebody. It may be the devil or it may be the Lord, but you're gonna have to serve somebody." We are always obeying something. When we obey the Holy Spirit, God is glorified and we are benefited. It's certainly always the very best choice.

4. What differences do you see between King Saul and King David?

There are so many differences between King Saul and Kind David. Perhaps as a group or with your accountability partner you can make a list comparing and contrasting these two men. Often times Saul is only remembered for how he turned from God, but before he turned he was God's anointed king. Study why King David did not end up like King Saul? How did they respond differently to sin? There's no one right answer here. Explore and allow the Holy Spirit to use the Bible to teach you truths as you compare these two very different people.

5. How does praising God, like David did in the Book of Psalms, help us live pure?

The problem with complaining is that it only makes your problems worse. When we bemoan our issues, we amplify their power and negativity. By keeping your eyes fixated on your sins, other people's sins, and all the things wrong with you and this world, you are only filling yourself with more hopelessness.

There is power in praising God because you to the exact opposite of what we just described. By putting your eyes on God, focusing on his perfections and beauty, you are de-amplifying the problems in your life and amplifying the source of the solution. When we praise God, we are reminding ourselves of the reality of his goodness and power to save. When we worship him, we are spurring ourselves on and giving us a hope that is rooted in our Savior.

Hebrews 12:2-3, ". . . looking to Jesus, the founder and perfecter of our faith, who for the joy that was set before him endured the cross, despising the shame, and is seated at the right hand of the throne of God.[3] Consider him who endured from sinners such hostility against himself, _so that you may not grow weary or fainthearted._"

When we look to Jesus and keep our thoughts fixated on him, this causes us to not grow weary and fainthearted. If we just look at our problems and neglect praising God, we will grow weary and fainthearted.

6. Read Romans 13:13-14. How does being in the presence of God relate to our ability to fight temptation?

Romans 13:13-14 (ESV), "Let us walk properly as in the daytime, not in orgies and drunkenness, not in sexual immorality and sensuality, not in quarreling and jealousy. But put on the Lord Jesus Christ, and make no provision for the flesh, to gratify its desires."

Romans 13:13-14 (NIV), "Let us behave decently, as in the daytime, not in carousing and drunkenness, not in sexual immorality and debauchery, not in dissension and jealousy. Rather, clothe yourselves with the Lord Jesus Christ, and do not think about how to gratify the desires of the flesh."

Romans 13:13-14 (NLT), "Because we belong to the day, we must live decent lives for all to see. Don't participate in the darkness of wild parties and drunkenness, or in sexual promiscuity and immoral living, or in quarreling and jealousy. Instead, clothe yourself with the presence of the Lord Jesus Christ. And don't let yourself think about ways to indulge your evil desires."

Fighting lust, porn, masturbation, sexual promiscuity, and all other forms of sexual immorality is twofold: running away from sin and running towards God. These Bible verses tell us that we are to avoid the practices associated with darkness while instead clothing ourselves with the presence of Jesus Christ. Being in the presence of Jesus affects every part of our being, including our mind. To avoid letting our minds drift to thinking about how to indulge our evil sexual desires, we must seek the presence of Jesus instead.

7. Read Psalm 101:1-4. What was one of David's techniques of avoiding sin?

Psalm 101:1-4, "I will sing of steadfast love and justice; to you, O LORD, I will make music. [2] *I will ponder the way that is blameless. Oh when will you come to me? I will walk with integrity of heart within my house;* [3] *I will not set before my eyes anything that is worthless. I hate the work of those who fall away; it shall not cling to me.* [4] *A perverse heart shall be far from me; I will know nothing of evil."*

It seems that David was committed not only to the avoidance of evil, but to the pursuit of praising and loving God. His primary motive was not just to not sin. The reason he desired not to sin was because he was so passionate about God.

King David said, "I will walk with integrity of heart within my house. I will not set before my eyes anything that is worthless. I hate the work of those who fall away; it shall not cling to me." I can't help but apply this Bible verse to the issue of pornography. How many times does porn use happen in the secrecy within our houses? David was committed to integrity not just when people were looking, but when he was within his own home. He knew God was always watching and he knew he must always be looking to God. Praise and worship is not just singing on Sunday morning in church. King David shows us that worship is a lifestyle that runs deep. It involves hating sin and loving God, even when no one is watching.

8. Read Psalm 16. What jumps out to you about this passage of Scripture?

Perhaps read this whole psalm as a small group Bible study or with your accountability partner. There are many powerful truths within this passage of Scripture that relate directly to the topics we are talking about in this Bible study.

One Bible verse that sticks out to me is Psalm 16:7, "I will praise the LORD, who counsels me; even at night my heart instructs me." Night time is an especially vulnerable time of the day when it comes to resisting sexual temptation. You are tired, often alone, and the canopy of darkness makes us feel like we can get away with more. King David combats this by praising God even throughout the night. It reminds me of Brother Lawrence, a man who spent his whole adult life "practicing the presence of God." He was a simple man with a simple life, but he decided to seek the presence of God as much as he possibly could. His life was transformed, and his journal writings and letters where later compiled into an amazing book that has helped countless people, "Practicing the Presence of God."

I also value the truth found in Psalm 16:8-9, "I keep my eyes always on the LORD. With him at my right hand, I will not be shaken. Therefore my heart is glad and my tongue rejoices; my body also will rest secure." Notice is was because King David kept his eyes on the Lord ("Therefore") that his heart was glad.

Psalm 51:11, "You make known to me the path of life; you will fill me with joy in your presence, with eternal pleasures at your right hand." The application of this Bible verse is obvious. If we hope to resist lustful sins we will need to know the path of life. We will need eternal pleasures, far greater and more motivating than these earthly pleasures that leave us wanting. All of this is found in the presence of God.

9. What do you fear losing if you continue to live in sexual sin?

Again, even though we can't lose our salvation, there are massive consequences to sexual sin. I know we have asked similar questions like this already, but it is imperative to keep before you the right motivation. We should fear losing our intimacy with God while also being motivated by gaining more intimacy with God. We should fear losing our marriage while also being motivated by the hope of having a better marriage. We should fear damaging our children while also being motivated by the hope of parenting healthy children who are growing in their love for the Lord as they watch us do the same.

Keep yourself motivated by reminding yourself often of what you can lose and what you can gain in this fight against lust.

10. Do you see the benefits of keeping a prayer journal? David wrote prayers to God about what was on his heart. Consider challenging yourself to write out prayers to the Lord like David. What prayer commitment do you feel led to make?

We've spent a lot of time studying the Psalms in this book. King David wrote most of these psalms. His journals should inspire us to do the same. Now look, I know not all of us are writers. Most of us can't write poetry like David could. But all of us are required to pray and were made to pray. A prayer journal helps us in a variety of ways: It helps keep your mind focused as you write, it allows you to remember what you've prayed, it gives you opportunities to look back and see God's answers to request you forgot you even made, it allows you to write Scripture which helps lodge it in your mind and heart, and on and on the benefits go.

With that said, we are all wired differently. Some of you pray better when you are walking, sitting in a quiet room, or praying over the Scriptures. Switch it up or do the same thing every day, the point is that you should seek to pray as much as you can. Don't feel ashamed that you don't pray one hour every day. But don't be content with praying one minute every day for the next fifty years. Keep seeking to grow. You may not be able to even conceive of praying for one hour straight, but if you start with ten minutes, and then next year challenge yourself with 20 minutes, and every year you keep growing in your prayer life, you will be amazed at how quickly your prayer life will be transformed. God loves a cheerful giver, therefore pray about what he is asking you to do in your prayer life and seek to do it joyfully.

Some of us need to start by praying about our prayer life. Ask God to give you the desire and the passion for prayer.

Going Deeper Chapter 8

1. Does it feel wrong to you to seek personal joy and pleasure from God? Does this ruin your motives in loving God?

Often times we think that the highest form of love is the love that is not motivated by anything that will benefit self. We think that to truly love, there must be zero self benefit or else our love is somehow tainted and lessoned.

This is a philosophical belief, not a biblical belief. God shows us that to have a personal affection and desire for someone is not a selfish love, it is a true love. If you don't desire your spouse, if you don't find satisfaction in your spouse, and if you don't benefit from his or her presence at all, your spouse will not feel more loved by you, he or she will feel less loved by you. One of the greatest forms of love is to allow yourself to need another person.

C.S. Lewis said it succinctly in regards to God's love for humans, "If He who in Himself can lack nothing, chooses to need us, it is because we need to be needed."

Additionally, it is not wrong to seek joy in the Lord because the Lord himself commands us to do this. In fact, to obey God, we must seek joy in him because, again, he commands us to find joy in him: "Delight yourself in the LORD. . . ." (Psalm 37:4), "Rejoice in the Lord always; again I will say, rejoice" (Philippians 4:4). Obedience and pursuing joy in the Lord are the same thing. If you are not seeking happiness in Christ, you are not obeying Christ.

Again, to find joy in God is simply to obey God. You can't glorify God if you don't find joy in God. As John Piper has said, "God is most glorified in us when we are most satisfied in him." Some call this "Christian Hedonism." For more on this deep and wonderful biblical truth, check out Piper's website, DesiringGod.org.

2. Why does King David pray that God would give him a willing spirit? Is God or King David in control of King David's will?

King David knows that he alone will be held responsible for his own behavior and his willingness or unwillingness to obey God. He also knows, however, that he was born flawed and thus needs God's Holy Spirit to correct in him all that is wrong, including his unwilling spirit.

Both facts coexist perfectly: Only God can cause us to produce good, and we are responsible for doing good. Theologically, this topic of God's sovereignty and man's free will has been hotly debated between two primary camps called Calvinism and Arminianism. There's too much to be said about what these two theological viewpoints believe. I have found, however, that no matter what side you find yourself on, there are at least two truths you must hold to if you call yourself a Bible believing Christian.

First, man (you, me, all of us) are responsible for our own sins. This means that God has never nor will ever directly cause sin or has sinned himself. Second, God alone is responsible for salvation. This means that man has never nor will ever save himself from his own sin. Both Arminians and Calvinists will explain in different ways how these two truths are accomplished. But if you claim something other than these two truths, you are going away from what Scripture holds. You can be a Christian with an Arminian or Calvinist perspective, but if you claim God is responsible for your sin or that you are responsible for your salvation, you are no longer stating a Christian perspective.

James 1:13-18, "Let no one say when he is tempted, "I am being tempted by God," for God cannot be tempted with evil, and he himself tempts no one. [14] _But each person is tempted when he is lured and enticed by his own desire_. [15] Then desire when it has conceived gives birth to sin, and sin when it is fully grown brings forth death. [16] Do not be deceived, my beloved brothers. [17] _Every good gift and every perfect gift is from above, coming down from the Father_ of lights with whom there is no variation or shadow due to change. [18] _Of his own will he brought us forth by the word of truth_, that we should be a kind of firstfruits of his creatures.

3. Does repentance involve just running away from sin, or does it also include running towards something better? (Romans 12:21, James 4:7)

Romans 12:21, "Do not be overcome by evil, but overcome evil with good.

James 4:7-8, "Submit yourselves therefore to God. Resist the devil, and he will flee from you. [8] Draw near to God, and he will draw near to you. Cleanse your hands, you sinners, and purify your hearts, you double-minded."

Put simply, we will never find God and live free by just avoiding evil; we must also pursue Christ. Of course to pursue God we must reject and abstain from sin. For as first Timothy 6:11 explains, "But as for you, O man of God, flee these things. Pursue righteousness, godliness, faith, love, steadfastness, gentleness." The fleeing, however, is not an end in itself. We are told to flee evil things so that we can "pursue" holiness in Jesus. We must refrain from evil so that we can pursue Christ. As good as it sounds, we are not to pursue Christ so that we can refrain from evil. Pursuit of Jesus is the real end goal. Refraining from evil is the means to a deeper relationship with God. A deeper relationship with God is not meant to be a means of refraining from evil.

The best way to be healthy is not to avoid eating junk food but to pursue eating healthy food. One must pursue a healthy diet or the hunger caused by a lack of food entirely will drive us to eat the quickest pleasure available which is usually very unhealthy. If our focus is only on what we can't eat, the hunger will overwhelm us because our bodies are meant to eat, to pursue food, to take it in, not to abstain. We don't grow healthy bodies by abstaining from unhealthy foods, we grow healthy by pursuing and eating healthy foods. We should avoid the junk only so we can eat the healthy. If we simply avoid the junk and forget to eat healthy, we are missing the point completely.

When Paul is instructing married people on how to avoid sexual temptation, he doesn't just say avoid all sexual sin; he instead says, "Do not deprive one another, except perhaps by agreement for a limited time, that you may devote yourselves to prayer; but then come together again, so that Satan may not tempt you because of your lack of self-control" (1

Corinthians 7:5). He tells us not to simply avoid sexual sin but to pursue holy sex with your spouse and prayer with God.

4. Do you feel more vulnerable to sexual temptation when you are tired? What can you do to avoid giving into temptation during these times of exhaustion?

As we have discussed through King David's prayer of repentance found in Psalm 51, humans often sexualize their feelings. Often times when we are tired we seek to find comfort through sexual sins. It's all too easy for a tired heart to find rest in the wrong places.

We need to prepare in advance so we don't enter into these times of total exhaustion where we are extremely vulnerable to the false comforts of lust, masturbation, adultery, and pornography. We must still fight even when we are extremely tired, but the better solution is to not let ourselves get this low. We are of course going to be tired in life, but we can guard against completely overdoing it to the point where we are sitting ducks for Satan's attacks.

Discuss amongst yourselves when you are most vulnerable. From personal experience and from talking to other pastors, oddly enough, many pastors are most vulnerable to sexual temptation in the times after they are done preaching. They put so much energy and effort into Sunday and the sermon, when it's all over and they are at home, they get slammed with exhaustion and many other attacks and temptations. A wise person prepares on how to handle this.

5. How does focusing on yourself hinder your ability to overcome sexual temptation?

Sexual sin is extremely selfish and self-centered. As we discussed earlier, God designed sex to be an expression of true, sacrificial love. Along with that, to really love your spouse, you must be vulnerable enough to need and enjoy her or him.

Sexual sin completely reverses what God intended and makes sex all about myself, me, and I. Sexual sin is the result of being self-centered. And sexual sin only perpetuates and deepens your self-centeredness. Trying to stop you selfishness by stopping your sexual sin is a good start, but it's better to first focus on your self-centeredness which will then help you stop your sexual sin. The way you address your selfishness is by not only looking at yourself less, but by looking to the Lord and his desires more.

Even when your intentions are good by analyzing your own internal problems, often times this self-introspection is a part of the problem. In our culture we have been taught to analyze and analyze and analyze ourselves. What's wrong with me? How am I feeling? What happened to me in my past? It's not wrong to ask these questions now and then. But life is not all about me, it's all about God. The more you focus on him, on his solutions, on his character, on his love for you, the faster you will be better off.

Don't be a problem-centered person. Be a Christ-centered person. You'll need to define what your problem really is, but you can't live there. Eventually you have to stop analyzing and thinking about yourself. Focus on God, read about God, pray to

God, and get out there and do something for the Kingdom of God.

6. Do you think it is significant that in each of Jesus' responses to Satan's temptations (Matthew 4:1-11), his answer began with "It is written"? Why or why not?

I do think this is very significant. Jesus didn't dialogue with the Devil. Jesus relied on God's word, believed God's word, proclaimed God's authority, and then "[Satan] departed from him until an opportune time" (Luke 4:13). Likewise, when we submit to God and fight Satan with Scripture, he will flee from us (James 4:7). Through our earthly lives Satan will seek to attack us at opportune times, but we have nothing to fear, for he who is in us is greater than he who is in the world (1 John 4:4).

Satan is like a seductive, evil woman. She masquerades with beauty and temptations, but what she really offers is death, "With much seductive speech she persuades him; with her smooth talk she compels him. All at once he follows her, as an ox goes to the slaughter" (Proverbs 7:21-22). It's worth noting that often times, when Jesus was casting out demons and one of them wanted to talk, "[Jesus] rebuked them and would not allow them to speak" (Luke 4:41).

Don't dialogue with the devil. Don't offer your thoughts and personal opinions. Don't ever listen to his crafty lies like those of an adulterous woman who breaks down her prey with "much seductive speech." To fight Satan: submit to God, believe the Bible, proclaim God's truth, speak only to God, listen only to God, let God's word speak on your behalf, and Satan will flee from you because he must listen to God.

We must fight Satan, but we must only fight Satan through the power of God proclaimed through his word.

(Note: I'm only talking about the regular temptations and spiritual warfare all Christians experience. Throughout the New Testament, Jesus rebuked demons out of people and spoke directly to them. Exorcism is a different topic entirely from what I am referring to in this section. Christian can be oppressed but they cannot be possessed since the Holy Spirit is in them, and where the Spirit of the Lord is there is liberty (2 Corinthians 3:17). Therefore, to use Jesus' exorcisms on non-Christians as a direct model to fight regular temptations that occur to Christians is not a good application of Scripture.)

7. Read Hebrews 12:1-3. What was Jesus' motivation? How should this affect the way we fight temptation?

Hebrews 12:1-3, "Therefore, since we are surrounded by so great a cloud of witnesses, let us also lay aside every weight, and sin which clings so closely, and let us run with endurance the race that is set before us, [2] looking to Jesus, the founder and perfecter of our faith, who for the joy that was set before him endured the cross, despising the shame, and is seated at the right hand of the throne of God.[3] Consider him who endured from sinners such hostility against himself, so that you may not grow weary or fainthearted."

Jesus' motivation was the "joy that was set before him." He did not endure the cross because he enjoyed suffering or because he was completely sterile of a desire for personal pleasure in God. No, Jesus went to the cross so that he could have pleasure in God. He despised the shame of the cross, but because he desired to sit at his Father's right hand and love his Father, he obeyed joyfully.

This passage of Scripture emphasizes the point we've been making throughout this chapter. In Hebrews 12:1, we are told to through off our sin. This means we are to run away from sin, repent of it, and forsake our old life. Hebrews 12:2, however, explains that we are also supposed to do what Jesus did, which was pursue the joy set before him. And Hebrews 12:3 again states that we are to consider what Jesus did, who endured suffering but also pursued satisfaction. To overcome sexual temptation, we need to avoid sin and pursue satisfaction in Christ.

8. What does it mean when the Bible says "the joy of the Lord is your strength" (Nehemiah 8:10)?

When you are at your job, when are you most productive? I don't know about you, but when I stay up late and then I'm dragging the next day, my production suffers. If I am angry about something, my production suffers. If am in a bad mood, my production suffers.

On the flipside, if I am having a good day, I am way more productive. The problem with all this is that life will always give you a reason to be mad, sad, or tired. Only God has the power and ability to give us joy in a broken world. Thus the joy of the Lord is our greatest source of strength. If you can be joyful in God despite difficult circumstances, you will always be strong. Your energy and strength will not be stolen by a world that is often joyless. The more joy we have in God, the more strength we will have to fight his battles, resist sexual temptation, and advance God's Kingdom.

9. How do God's sovereignty and your free will connect? How does God's authority empower our freedom rather than take away our freedom?

Before God saved us, we were slaves to sin. Our wills freely chose to obey our master, which was sin. When God redeemed us through the gospel of Jesus Christ, he set our will free. Now we have the ability to obey our new master, which is God. God doesn't negate our free will, he sets our will free. He does not force us to love him, he now empowers us to love him. We can't do it without him. Now we can do it through him.

God doesn't force his love on us and he does not force us to love him. With that said, it would be impossible for the human heart to love God without God the Holy Spirit empowering it. God initiates our love for him (John 6:44), God give us the desire to love him (Philippians 2:13), and God gives us the power to love him (Galatians 5:22).

God freely justifies us. This means that he makes us holy, righteous, and literally transfers the perfections of Christ onto us. Sanctification, however, is the lifelong process of learning to live out what God has already made you and given you. Justification is done to us. Sanctification includes our willingness to participate in our growth.

For example: The Father has given us the Holy Spirit so we can understand the Scriptures. If you choose not to read your Bible, however, you are not going to grow in knowledge. The Father has given us the Holy Spirit to produces the fruits of the Spirit, which includes love. But if we choose not to be "led by the Spirit" we will not produces this fruit as much as we could have, "I say, walk by the Spirit, and you will not gratify the desires of the flesh" (Galatians 5:16).

God is the only reason you can produce a real love for God. But you must still participate and actively choose to walk in the Spirit, to obey God, not backslide, and love God.

10. Rest doesn't just happen. We have to make time to rest. Take a few moments to write down your weekly schedule. Where can you make time to intentionally rest in the Lord?

When you want to go on vacation, do you tell your boss that day, leave for a week, get in your car and just go? Of course not! You need to plan your vacation weeks and even months before it actually takes place. The more responsibility you have, the more planning you will need to find rest.

When you are a young adult with little responsibilities, the planning necessary to find rest is a lot less. You still need to plan, but like going on vacation, you can make this happen a lot easier when you have less of the responsibilities of full adulthood.

When you have a spouse, a family, people working under your authority, and when you have all the good responsibilities that come with maturity, going on vacation is not as simple as it once was. You need to consider where your spouse and kids will want to go too, so just picking the spot will be much harder. You need to get the kids set for missing school, you need to get them packed, you need to find arrangements for the dog, you need to budget better since you are taking multiple people, and on and on the planning will need to go.

Likewise, on a day to day level, the more responsibility you have, the more intentional you will need to be about planning your rest time in the Lord.

The solution to our walk with God is not to have less responsibility. The solution is being mature enough to rightly handle the blessing of having much responsibility. Don't let your busy schedule be an excuse. If you want to be free from sexual sin, you are going to have to prioritize your life accordingly so you will have the rest and time necessary to cultivate a healthy walk with God and with those who are dear to you.

Going Deeper Chapter 9

1. What's the danger of emphasizing good works without emphasizing God's grace (Ephesians 2:8-10)?

Ephesians 2:8-10, "For by grace you have been saved through faith. And this is not your own doing; it is the gift of God, [9] not a result of works, so that no one may boast. [10] For we are his workmanship, created in Christ Jesus for good works, which God prepared beforehand, that we should walk in them."

2 Timothy 2:9 (NIV), "He has saved us and called us to a holy life—not because of anything we have done but because of his own purpose and grace."

Philippians 3:8-9, "For his sake I have suffered the loss of all things and count them as rubbish, in order that I may gain Christ [9] and be found in him, not having a righteousness of my own that comes from the law, but that which comes through faith in Christ, the righteousness from God that depends on fait…"

The gospel of Jesus Christ is different than every other religion because it is not based in what the human must do. Christianity is based in what God has done on behalf of the sinner. All worldly religions prove they were made by man because they are dependent upon what man can do for himself. They all require people to appease a god or a code of living. Christianity alone is based on putting your faith in a Savior who already accomplished your salvation. Grace is what makes Christianity different.

When Christians emphasize good works without placing good works in their proper, biblical context, we run the risk of losing the whole point of the gospel and becoming like every other worldly religion.

2. What's the danger of emphasizing God's grace without emphasizing good works (Ephesians 2:8-10)?

Ephesians 2:8-10, "For by grace you have been saved through faith. And this is not your own doing; it is the gift of God, [9] not a result of works, so that no one may boast. [10] For we are his workmanship, created in Christ Jesus for good works, which God prepared beforehand, that we should walk in them."

Titus 2:14 (NIV), "[Jesus] gave himself for us to redeem us from all wickedness and to purify for himself a people that are his very own, eager to do what is good.

James 2:14-18, "What good is it, my brothers, if someone says he has faith but does not have works? Can that faith save him? [15] If a brother or sister is poorly clothed and lacking in daily food, [16] and one of you says to them, "Go in peace, be warmed and filled," without giving them the things needed for the body, what good is that? [17] So also faith by itself, if it does not have works, is dead. [18] But someone will say, "You have faith and I have works." Show me your faith apart from your works, and I will show you my faith by my works."

It seems in church history, trends swing back and forth like a pendulum or a grandfather clock. I am currently 30 years old. There was a time, when my parents were young, that churches throughout America were extremely dogmatic and legalistic. In response to that, my parents' generation experienced a ground swell of churches who emphasized the great love, mercy, and compassion of God. Much revival and good happened because of this.

Unlike my parents' generation, I grew up in a time were the majority of churches (from my personal experience) emphasized the love and grace of God almost exclusively. It seems that churches felt people had been taught so much about the wrath and fear of God from the generation prior, most people needed to hear about God's mercy and love. Although much good happened, as a result, those who grew up from childhood in this environment (like many of my peers and I) never heard about the judgment of God. Therefore many Christians around my age have grown up thinking that no matter what they do, God is always smiling down on them. They interpret "God's unconditional love" as an unconditional excuse to completely disobey him.

Because of a fear that people will think they have to earn their salvation, Bible verses like Hebrews 13:4 are simply not preached too often, "Let marriage be held in honor among all, and let the marriage bed be undefiled, for God will judge the sexually immoral and adulterous."Bible verses like this do not mean that we will earn or lose salvation from God based upon our sexual morality or immorality. But Hebrews 13:4, and verse like this, point to the great importance of good works being present in the believer's life.

The Bible makes clear that those who think they have faith but it is not accompanied by good works are only fooling themselves. The danger of never teaching the biblical truth regarding good works is that people think they are saved when they are really not. We are certainly not saved by our good works. We are saved by grace and through faith alone. But when you truly put your faith in Jesus, your life will then produce good works (not perfection).

As James said, ". . . I will show you my faith by my works" (James 2:18). Ephesians 2:8-10 is a great example of what we're talking about. Oftentimes preachers today only read Ephesians 2:8-9. But if you don't experience Ephesians 2:10, then this means you have not truly experiences Ephesians 2:8-9. None of us will be perfect, but if your life has not changed at all since you have become a Christian and you have no good works in your life, the Bible says you are not truly saved.

3. Do you find yourself trying to do what God desires because he loves you or so that he will love you? Do you think there is a difference?

In our moments of weakness and when we lack clarity, every Christian has experienced the desire to work for God so he will love and forgive us. When we are thinking clearly and biblically though, we will seek to serve God not so he will love us but because we know that he does love us.

There is a giant difference between the two. When you try to serve God so he will love you, you are operating in a works-based theology that is not supported in Scripture. When you are seeking to serve God because he does love you and because you know he as truly saved you, you are then exemplifying the fruit that accompanies a healthy, growing Christian faith.

The external will often look the same in both instances. Therefore it is crucial that we have an honest look at our own heart and motivations. We must spend time in God's word and in prayer so the Holy Spirit will correct us when we begin to have false motives. No one has the right to judge your motives except you and God. Likewise, no one will be held responsible for your lack of good motives except you before God.

4. If someone was to ask you to help them overcome their sexual sin, what would be your first thought? Often our first thought is evidence of what we are letting define us. Are you defined by your past sins or are you defined by your Savior? What's holding you back from helping others?

We must be brutally honest with ourselves and God. There's no shame in admitting that you are not ready to help others be free from sins like lust, porn, masturbation, and forms of sexual immorality. If you are actively struggling with these sins, it's best to keep focusing on your fight before you begin to help others.

With that said, you don't need to be an expert, a catholic saint, a seminary student, or a mega church pastor to feel like you are able to help others overcome sexual temptation. If God has grown you and taught you how to love him while avoiding sexual sins (not perfectly), then God expects you to share with others what he has given to you.

When you have truly received God's grace and forgiven yourself too, then you will no longer feel like a hypocrite when you help others. So pray about what is holding you back. Confess your sins, repent, mourn for a period of time, but then move on.

God's grace cost him too much for us to not fully enjoy it and share it with others.

5. Read 2 Corinthians 1:8-12. How do Paul's past experiences with God give him confidence in the present? How can our past experiences of grace help us in the present?

2 Corinthians 1:8-12, "For we do not want you to be unaware, brothers, of the affliction we experienced in Asia. For we were so utterly burdened beyond our strength that we despaired of life itself. [9] Indeed, we felt that we had received the sentence of death. But that was to make us rely not on ourselves but on God who raises the dead. [10] He delivered us from such a deadly peril, and he will deliver us. On him we have set our hope that he will deliver us again. [11] You also must help us by prayer, so that many will give thanks on our behalf for the blessing granted us through the prayers of many. [12] For our boast is this, the testimony of our conscience, that we behaved in the world with simplicity and godly sincerity, not by earthly wisdom but by the grace of God, and supremely so toward you."

Paul has history with God. This passage speaks about persecution he endured which only made him trust God more once he went through it. Likewise, all of our experiences of God's faithfulness should cause the same results in us.

6. What similarities do you see between Psalm 51 and Psalm 40?

Psalm 40:2-3, "He drew me up from the pit of destruction, out of the miry bog, and set my feet upon a rock, making my steps secure. [3] He put a new song in my mouth, a song of praise to our God. *Many will see and fear, and put their trust in the* L*ORD*."

Psalm 51:14-15, "Deliver me from bloodguiltiness, O God, O God of my salvation, and my tongue will sing aloud of your righteousness.[15] *O Lord, open my lips, and my mouth will declare your praise."*

Here is an example of David praising God for what God has done. David didn't praise God so God would move on his behalf. David's worship was a response to God's awesome power.

Psalm 40:6, "In sacrifice and offering you have not delighted, but you have given me an open ear. Burnt offering and sin offering you have not required."

Psalm 51:16-17, "For you will not delight in sacrifice, or I would give it; you will not be pleased with a burnt offering.[17] *The sacrifices of God are a broken spirit; a broken and contrite heart, O God, you will not despise."*

God does not desire sacrifices on our behalf to pay for our sins. He desires a changed life and a contrite heart in response to his sacrifice for our sins.

7. How does humility help us teach and love others?

Pride repels people and God.

Psalm 138:6, "For though the LORD is high, he regards the lowly, but the haughty he knows from afar."

James 4:6, "God opposes the proud, but gives grace to the humble."

2 Timothy 2:24-25, "And the Lord's servant must not be quarrelsome but kind to everyone, able to teach, patiently enduring evil, [25] correcting his opponents with gentleness."

People will not listen to your counsel until they first know you care. Prideful people care about themselves. To be a great teacher, leader, or counselor, humility will be one of your greatest assets. Additionally, it's difficult to go to someone for help when you feel they cannot understand your situation. Humility allows you to share your personal struggles which God has caused you to overcome, which drops people's defenses and helps them confide in you. We need to be careful not to share too much, but when people see you as someone who has never struggled with addictive sins or lust, then it will be less likely they seek your help and receive your counsel.

Psalm 51:17 states that God wants us to have "a broken and contrite heart."This does not only mean that God wants us to be humbled and broken in the sense that we are wrecked over our sins. It's good to go through a period of brokenness over your sins. But after we forgiven and it's right to nmove on, God wants us to be "broken" like a wild horse is broken, meaning we are obedient to our master.

8. If God doesn't need our good works, why does he use us to produce good works for him?

Right from the beginning of creation, God made man to work the garden (Genesis 2:15). God could have worked it himself, *but he used Adam to do it. God told Adam and Eve to be fruitful and multiply (Genesis 1:28). He could have populated the earth by producing people himself as he did with the first man and woman, but instead he chose to use Adam and Eve to produce other people. God could have made the ark, but God used Noah to do it. He could have struck down Goliath, but he used David to cast the stone. God could have set the infant Jesus in the manger himself, but he used Mary's body to host the Savior and Joseph's fatherly care to guide Mary and Jesus along in the early years. Jesus could have stayed to make disciples throughout the earth, but he commissioned the eleven and all of us to do it through his power.*

God has ordained humans to be used as his tool to accomplish his will. It is a profound mystery how God brings about his will through the free will of man, but he does it nonetheless. Only a real God could produce this feat. If you could fully understand everything about God, he would not be God.

God uses people for many reasons. One reason is that it is an act of love for him to do this for us. God knows that the best life possible for humans is a life of serving God. If we had no purpose given to us by God, God would not be loving us the best way possible.

9. Why do you think it is so important that we not only seek to find freedom from sexual sins ourselves, but that we also seek to help others do the same?

The second greatest command in all of Scripture is to love people (Matthew 22:36-40). To love God well, we must love others well. God's image, though broken, is stamped on every human that walks the planet. From those in prison to those in the womb, God cares about them. Because each person is human, they deserve the opportunity to experience the gospel and be treated with dignity. This does not mean that consequences should be avoided, but it does mean that for God's sake, we should offer every human certain rights.

Discipleship is one of God's commands to all Christians. He wants us all reproducing ourselves. When he gives us redemption, he expects us to help others receive redemption as well.

Also, when you take the time to teach someone, you are taking the next step forward in your own growth as well. When you are required to explain something to someone else, it requires you to go even deeper with your own understanding. When you lead others, you will be forced to look at your own life even closer. Teaching others will help you grow and learn more.

10. Even if you are actively struggling in certain areas of your sexuality while also seeking to repent, God has still shown you grace and love. If you have made progress and are no longer committing the sexual sins you once did, certainly you have good news to share with others. In either case, write out some of the blessings God has shown you that you can share with other people who may be struggling like you have in the past.

Again, even if you are in the midst of struggling with your sexual sins, you can at least share with others how God is still with you, being faithful to you in the midst of your struggle. You can tell people how faithful God has been to you and how he continues to lead you down the right path no matter how many times you get off course.

As we've stated throughout this chapter, if you are bit further down the road, it's time for you to disciple others now. You have so much to share with others. You may just need to organize your thoughts so you can feel better prepared to share them with those you know are in need like you once were.

Going Deeper Chapter 10

1. What are your immediate reactions to this chapter? What parts do you agree and disagree with? Why?

Some of the topics that were discussed in this chapter have been hotly debated by Christians. Some believe, for example, that every sexual sin, down to the thoughts in the mind, should be confessed to your spouse. Some believe that you won't be forgiven if you don't confess your sin directly to the person you sinned against, so they would counsel you to call every ex-girlfriend or ex-boyfriend you have had and confess the sins you now realize you committed against them and with them.

As you can tell from this chapter, I have a different view. God is the one who forgives sins. There is certainly a time and place to apologize and ask for forgiveness from those you've sinned against. Matthew 5:23-24, "So if you are offering your gift at the altar and there remember that your brother has something against you, [24] leave your gift there before the altar and go. First be reconciled to your brother, and then come and offer your gift."

With that said, we must be wise in how we approach confessing sexual sins, "Let no corrupting talk come out of your mouths, but only such as is good for building up, as fits the occasion, that it may give grace to those who hear" (Ephesians 4:29). Each of us will need to pray about what words "fits the occasion, that it may give grace to those who hear."

When it comes to contacting people from your past, often times it's just not wise. God is the one who forgives sin.

Embrace that truth. Pray that other people will forgive you and that you will forgive others, and trust God's power to completely redeem.

2. How has your sexual sin hurt other people, directly and indirectly?

By this time, if you are working through this Bible study on Psalm 51 with an accountability partner or small group of men or women, hopefully by now you have grown in your relationships with one another. Be vulnerable and share the damaging effects of your sexual sins. Have you cheated, hurt your spouse by your porn addiction, or been absent from your family because of your hardened heart? If you are not married, how is your masturbation not only hurting you, but other people too? How does your selfishness end up hurting others?

The less you are walking with God, the more you are missing his plan for you. God's plan for our lives always involves loving and serving other people. When we are lost in lust, we are not available to help those we are supposed to be serving.

3. Why do you think God doesn't always save us from consequences even though he always forgives us?

There is a biblical difference between punishment and discipline. Punishment is given with the intent of getting the offender to pay for what they did wrong. Discipline is done with the intent of correcting negative, hurtful behavior. God spares us of punishment through his grace, but he does not spare us of discipline because he loves us.

Hebrews 12:5-6, 11, "My son, do not regard lightly the discipline of the Lord, nor be weary when reproved by him.[6] For the Lord disciplines the one he loves, and chastises every son whom he receives . . .[11] For the moment all discipline seems painful rather than pleasant, but later it yields the peaceful fruit of righteousness to those who have been trained by it."

Additionally, one day God will deliver all Christians from every consequence of sin when we are redeemed completely through the resurrection of our bodies. When we are living on the new earth, all the old consequences of sin will be no more.

4. Why should every Christian seek to forgive those who have sinned against them?

Matthew 6:14-15, "[14] For if you forgive others their trespasses, your heavenly Father will also forgive you, [15] but if you do not forgive others their trespasses, neither will your Father forgive your trespasses."

Ephesians 4:32, "Be kind to one another, tenderhearted, forgiving one another, as God in Christ forgave you."

We don't earn our forgiveness from God when we forgive others. Rather, when we forgive others, it proves we have truly received God's forgiveness and transformation. 1 John 4:20, "If anyone says, 'I love God,' and hates his brother, he is a liar; for he who does not love his brother whom he has seen cannot love God whom he has not seen."

5. Why is it so hard to love our enemies? What's one lesson you have learned from King David on how to treat your enemy?

King David showed his true character when he spared King Saul. Throughout David's life, one of the ways he exhibited his love for God was through his respect for other people, even those who sought his harm. King David tried to leave justice in the hands of God.

It's so hard to do this because forgiving and loving our enemies is where our Christianity is really tested. As C.S. Lewis said, "Everyone thinks forgiveness is a lovely idea until he has something to forgive."

Jesus said in Matthew 5:43-48, "You have heard that it was said, 'You shall love your neighbor and hate your enemy.' [44] But I say to you, Love your enemies and pray for those who persecute you, [45] so that you may be sons of your Father who is in heaven. For he makes his sun rise on the evil and on the good, and sends rain on the just and on the unjust. [46] For if you love those who love you, what reward do you have? Do not even the tax collectors do the same? [47] And if you greet only your brothers, what more are you doing than others? Do not even the Gentiles do the same? [48] You therefore must be perfect, as your heavenly Father is perfect."

As we've discussed, Christ justifies us and makes us perfect, but we are also in the process of being sanctified as we learn to live a life that is being perfected more and more in Christ. One indicator for perfection is complete forgiveness of your enemies. God forgave us when we were still his enemies

(Romans 5:8) because he is perfect. We can know how far along the process of sanctification we really are by looking at how quickly and thoroughly we forgive others who have sinned against us.

6. Why is prayer so essential when it comes to forgiveness and inner healing?

The heart belongs to God. He's in control, he's the expert, and only he has the power to transform us at the heart level. If someone won't forgive you, the best and only option is to pray for them. When you are struggling to forgive another, the best and only option is to pray. Certainly pray from your heart, but also pray the Scriptures. Pray over passages like Psalm 103 that explain the great mercy of God so that you might act like him through his power.

Romans 8:26-27 states, "Likewise the Spirit helps us in our weakness. For we do not know what to pray for as we ought, but the Spirit himself intercedes for us with groanings too deep for words. And he who searches hearts knows what is the mind of the Spirit, because the Spirit intercedes for the saints according to the will of God."

When a situation seems hopeless, or your inner wounds just seem too deep to ever be healed, most of the time it will be difficult to find the words to pray. But pray nonetheless. Sit before the Lord with your greatest hurts, ask him to heal you, and the Holy Spirit will intercede in ways that no one can describe with words. I'd love to completely explain healing prayer, but I simply can't. The best thing I can say is: It really does work!

God's power is real, so don't neglect connecting with him in prayer. He desires to heal and restore, and so often these gifts come through times of deep prayer and intimacy with the Lord who loves you immensely. Prayer is not always about words. It's about being in the presence of the Lord.

7. Read Psalm 51:16 and Psalm 51:19. Why does God not delight in burnt offerings in Psalm 51:16 but does delight in them in Psalm 51:19? What's the difference between how these sacrifices are offered?

Psalm 51:16-19, "For you will not delight in sacrifice, or I would give it; you will not be pleased with a burnt offering. [17] The sacrifices of God are a broken spirit; a broken and contrite heart, O God, you will not despise. [18] Do good to Zion in your good pleasure; build up the walls of Jerusalem; [19] then will you delight in right sacrifices, in burnt offerings and whole burnt offerings; then bulls will be offered on your altar."

Psalm 51:17 speaks of having a humble heart. Psalm 51:18 is a request that only God could do. Perhaps David is saying that God doesn't delight in sacrifices that are based in our righteousness or our desire to cleanse ourselves of sin through our sacrifices. Perhaps David is saying that God delights in sacrifices that are given with humility, in thanksgiving, knowing that God alone can save.

These verses do not contradict and David is not telling his people who lived under Old Testament law to contradict the law by not giving God the sacrifices he commands. David is simply expressing the truth that if our hearts are not right, our external obedience to the law is worthless in God's eyes. Psalm

51:16-19 is David saying that he knows God doesn't just want a religious sacrifice, he wants David's heart and motives to be right. When God gives David this right frame of heart (Psalm 51:16-18), "Then" (Psalm 51:19) will God delight in David's external sacrifices.

The same is true for all of us. God doesn't just want you to read the Bible, serve the poor, and go to church. He won't delight in these things if your heart is not right in doing him. But when your heart is right, "then" he will delight in these sacrifices too. God's not saying to ignore the external commands, he is just saying that if we ignore our hearts, then our external sacrifices for God don't delight him.

8. Do you believe a husband and wife should be each other's daily/regular/primary accountability partner? If one spouse struggles with porn or masturbation, how often do you think he or she should communicate about this with the other spouse?

I don't believe spouses should be each other's regular accountability partners for a variety of reasons discussed in this chapter. However, I do believe your spouse needs to know what you struggle with. I know this can feel like a tightrope act, so you will have to pray about what the Lord is leading you to do.

My best counsel is to have a conversation about what you both feel should be shared. Honestly, your wife or husband probably doesn't want to know everything on a daily bases. But he or she will want to know certain things. Set clear boundaries and expectations. Perhaps your spouse will want to know every time you sin by using porn, but perhaps she won't want to know every time you lust about a woman on a commercial you saw during the football game. Talk it out and follow through.

Anytime your sexual sin involves another person in the flesh other than your spouse, it's an absolute that you must tell your spouse.

9. List everyone you believe your sexual sin has hurt. Pray about if you should contact any of these people to apologize to or if you should simply pray for their healing.

Consult the advice I gave at the beginning of Chapter 10. A good rule of thumb when deciding how to help others heal from the ways you've hurt them is by asking yourself: What will be the fruit of me contacting them?

If you feel the fruit (result) will be a weight being lifted off their shoulders, closure they desperately need, or an opportunity for them to defend their side of the story that you never let them share, then it's probably best to contact that person. If, for example, contacting someone is only going to anger the new boyfriend or girlfriend, stir up a big fight, or reignite a toxic relationship you know you're not strong enough to resist, then keep your distance. Perhaps write a letter with no return address when necessary.

Pray about what the Lord is leading you to do and obey.

10. Write out a prayer of protection and healing for your marriage (or future marriage). Ask God to protect your

marriage from sexual sin, heal your marriage from the sexual sin, and grow your marriage so both you and your spouse will be able to love each other well and enjoy God together. (If you feel God has led you to live a celibate life, pray about this instead.)

Pour your heart out to God. Pray to him. God loves you and has all the power. God wants you to live free and he is ready to supply you will all that you will need to glorify him. So get praying!

Made in the USA
Middletown, DE
25 January 2022

59632550R00149